Langmythics

Language+mystery+Theos+Mathematics

K Sabota

Magister of Logos
Solux Universum

Dedication

This book is dedicated to
those who
thought+**link**]**th**ink.
see+**ask**]**se**ek and
quest+**sho**wn]question
Y

ISBN-13: 978-0-9816383-7-9

Table of Contents

Preface: How this Book Evolved.

In second grade, there were ABC letter cards above the blackboard of pictures which were related to the letters. The "i" was an Indian brave with a feather dot above his head, the M was two mountain peaks, the S was a snake etc. Years later after haven written poetry and books. I realized that similar objects may in fact be related to their original usage in an ancient symbolic proto-language. I also I noticed that some words were related by sound although they were spelled differently and not near each other in the dictionary, because the dictionary only organizes words based on spelling, not sound and logic relationships. For example, the words "know and gnosis" are clearly related by sound and meaning but are not found near each other in the dictionary.

I began writing the related words down onto a large posterboard that I could connect with lines, erase, move and circle, like a mind map. I connected groups of words together as "word families" that have parts of words that are in other words and or words that had similar but not exact spellings. When this grew too large, I put them into a computer document.

I then began to write alliterated poems with the word families which revealed that letters had personalities, functions or meanings unto themselves. I also noticed each letter had archaic sound-shape associations, and some additive mathematical relationships like acrostic acronyms such as UFO and NASA etc. I then made a letter multiplication table (see table page 89) to try to see a graphic of how sounds were functioning. After accumulating many poems, I then arranged them and published book called "The Hidden Sword: A Puzzle Mist Story". (Available on Amazon)

While thinking about how to put acouple of the poems on social media, I realized that I could circle and draw connections to the fragments of words to show how they related within the poem. This then led me to engineer mathematical word equations to show how words are composed of fragments and sometimes whole words are nested in other words. After posting some of my ideas into traditional linguistics forums, my ideas were rejected and I realized that what I was doing was not traditional Linguistics but a new approach, so I named it Langmathics. I then because there were no historical facts to support my work, I combined Langmathic with the mystery of myth and renamed it Langmythics

Langmythic word equations reverse engineers and divides words into fragments then finds separate logical words that contain those fragments. This technique helps decipher what the meaning of groups of related words reveal.

So, after developing this method I took all the alliterated poems from The Hidden Sword book and reduced and rearranged them by common themes and condensed them using this Langmythic technique

These Langmathic divisions of words and the interpretations are speculative and sometimes two different combinations of words make sense for the same word. The reader is invited to propose alternative more logical possible words.

The second half of this book is a

Language+**fract**+**fact**+**make**]Langfractic

Fractal+**sh**own+lib**rary**]Fractionary". This is an alphabetical arrangement of Langmythic fractmathic words that highlight in bold the logical fragments of words that combine to form other words. The Fractionary is a work in progress and will be improved, corrected or expanded as necessary.

Acknowledgements

I thank the information that I have received in an ancient cryptic book that I was given in a dream.

What is Fractmathic Langmythics?

What is **Fra**cture+**math**+mag**ic**] Fractmathic
Language+(**my**stery+**Theos**)**myth**+mag**ic**]Langmythics?
"In the beginning was the Word, and the Word was God". The
spelling of words are **sp**eak+**tell**]spells. Each letter has an
individual meaning. Letters combined with other letters have a
new combined meaning and then combine with other letters to
make words. Then sometimes two words combined together to
make a new word. Langmythics uses fractmathics to fracture
words apart into complete separate words and then highlights with
Bold Type which fractions parts of the words have been
mathematically added together to create the original word. This
technique can show how many other words are connected and
related like portmanteaus.

Modern linguistics trace word evolution though written
etymological evidence and historical research to determine origin
and meaning but ultimately, linguistics comes to a dead end when
it gets back to pre-writing of mankind.
language+**ma**tter+**Theos**+**magic**]Langmathics reverse engineers'
words and breaks them into fragment parts that can be either
abstract, artistic, false cognate mathematical mathmatchical
relationships of word sounds.

These relationships might be from a prehistoric protolanguage
based on nature observation or coincidental vibrational fractures
of sound. Langmythics can be called a pseudo-science because it
has no historically provable evidence other than it makes logical
sense derived by direct visual and sound experience.

In the beginning of mankind's speech development, the first
sounds would have defined natural materials and actions that
were most important relative to day-to-day life and survival. These
would be sky, nature, food, sex related words. Perhaps observing
star constellations (>leads to) imagination> images> pictures>
graphics> symbols> letters> words> sentences> thoughts>
concepts> books> knowledge> action> power> numbers>
money> government computers> AI>?. As time passed and
people migrated, these word sounds would be slurred together
and mispronounced to make new spoken words. Eventually some
words would become pictographic symbols written in dirt or
carved on stones. Some of this primitive evidence would be lost
to time. Eventually, paper, ink and carved hieroglyphic symbols

were invented to represent the objects and actions. Then letters came to represent symbols and these letters were combined into nouns and verbs spelled differently by many different people. Finally, words were added together to make sentences and then paragraphs, made chapters, made books. Language and spelling were a fluid and evolving from person to person through generations and cultures. Then in an effort to standardize communications, dictionaries were invented that dictated what was correct spelling. These spellings were not all logical or phonetic. Then grammar was invented which generally standardized sentence structure systems. Then linguistics evolved to historically research previous writings like word fossils to prove where words evolved from. Although dictionarys and linguistics standardizations are necessary for the advancement communication, our language is treated as a science that is based solely on history with a hierarchy of experts that control it and decide what is correct.

The standardization of Illogical non-phonetic spellings, and alphabetical order of dictionaries has obscured and disguised some words sound relationships because those words are not found near each other in the dictionary.

Langmythics approaches spelling and word relationships by reverse engineering, and dividing words based on function, logic and additive structures. Like fractal portmanteaus, acronyms and compound words, Langmythics reveals how parts of words logically connect more like fractured puzzle pieces and logically support the original word's definition.

Langmathics view sounds of words as not only material symbolic letters, but mathematical vibrations that exist in the invisible ether long before writing began. Sounds and words could exist and travel from population to population with no trace of how they traveled or come from the cosmos and manifested like numbers did to different cultures.

To deny the possibility of langmythics is a suppression of the gnosis of an undeniable logic relationship of words. It is time to recognize langmythics as a new branch of language study that is a forward exploration of language that offers new possibilities of how words have come to be, or could become and evolve. It is a way to see language as a living code of communication instead of only a historical investigation of etymology. Imagine if we studied math only based on the proof of numbers mentioned in texts rather than how numbers actually function. It would be absurd.

To be open to understanding Langmythics we must understand that "absolutely correct" spellings of many words is nothing more than dictated fabrications of the dictionary. Sound can be reduced to vibration which can be represented mathematically which is truer than illogical spellings dictated by the dictionary. Language is vibrations and vibrations are mathematical, therefore Language is mathematical.

Langmythics logically decodes words using spelling and phonetic sounds of various accents and languages.

As of this writing, Langmythics is at its early stage of development and is a is a poetic artwork that arranges word fragments to fit into related themes. However, it is believed that with the help of and AI program, a 3D mind-map like picture will eventually be able to be constructed showing how all sounds of words are connected.

Although any fool can see many words sounds clearly fit together logically, only a "phool" would dispute the obvious evidence of Langmythics, because to do so would be denying the logical fit of word fragments solely because there is no historical evidence that these pieces fit together.

Writing Symbol Key

Bold text word parts are added together with + signs to equal (Sub Sum words) + other logical words parts and /alternative choices to show the final] Total Sum Word.

Bold   Text indicates what word letters are added together.
+   Shows what **bold** letters to add together.
/ ...   Means "or" of two alternative logical word choices
(..)   Shows Sub Sum words in the equation
]   Is an equal's sign = shows the final Total Sum Word

Explanation of a Langmythic Word Equation

Add **BOLD** parts of words to equal
Sub Sum Words and Total Sum Words

Ar or Au+Thor = Author+rit or ri...t + **e** = Authority

(**Arch**/gold/**AU+Thor**)**Author**+write/**right**+be]Authority

     Sub Sum Word   Total Sum Word

Letter Sound & Shape Connection Theory

Through writing of The Hidden Sword: A Puzzle Poem Mist Story, I discovered that each letter of the English alphabet has tendencies or functions based on sound and shape symbols of individual letters and logical spelling connections that are not taught in our current English language school systems.

To understand these theories the reader must think beyond previously documented school and dictionary learning. Realize that we don't totally understand what spelling is. We can question why each letter is shaped the way it is and why letters are combined in certain ways. For example, was the A shaped pointing up because it pointed to things Above? Could the letter P be shaped to match the puff force that comes out of the mouth as an indication of a powerful purpose?

A reader's immediate reaction may be to think of words that do not fit into the theories. But remember; these theories are tendencies not dictating absolute laws and our speech is very ancient and has morphed through many languages and cultures over time, so of course not all words will fit. In fact, I present multiple theories for some letter meanings.

If we analyze the evolution spelling, we see it began as an attempt to make symbols for sounds. This started by pictographs and hieroglyphics. Eventually wise wizards and witty witches began using planetary symbols to represent different processes such as condensation or distillation to record the alchemical experiments and potion recipes. Each symbol represented a different process and they would write them down in order as formulas. This is why they said that witches casted spells because they used an early form of symbolic spelling. Today we have updated names for witches and wizards; to the socially acceptable terms of doctors, scientists, mathematicians and chemists.

Eventually many forms of letters shapes began to evolve. How and why are letters shaped in specific ways? Did their shapes originally have meaning unto themselves? This we can now only speculate because it was pre-history from many various cultures. That is why this book contains the word myth as mystery.

In early cultures it was the priests who had more free time to devote to become learned readers and writers and were the early developers of our modern letter word system. Were they part of a conspiracy to hide word connections with silent letters, letters with multiple sounds, and similar sounding words spelled differently? Why did they create only one symbol letter for each vowel although each vowel has many different sounds? We do know that spelling in antiquity was not an exact science and travelers with different accents pronounced the same word slightly different causing the same word to be recorded differently by a different people. We also know that some words were deliberately spelled different so that the reader would know/no which version of the word was being used. We have modern evidence that the spelling of many names were changed by mistake when immigrants passed through Ellis Island New York.

Now our modern-day spelling has become regulated by teachers enforcing the dictates of the dictionary which arranges phonetically illogical spellings by alphabetical order rather than pronunciation and sound families. For example, we will not find the words "know" and "gnosis" near each other in the dictionary. Although stabilization of spelling in a dictionary has been overall good, because we can all use a standardized system and this has led to the majority of people now being readers. But in another way, we have been indoctrinated that one way of organizing and spelling is right and have locked correctness in time and stopped the evolution of spelling. Modern man thinks that our written communication is highly evolved, but evolution does not stand still.

We can reconnect spelling to sound and shape function and build a new mind map of meaning. We can learn to see the spelling of words more mathematically, like how letters of an acrostic that add together to make a word. You will see words as more containing artifacts of archaic treasury of original fragments of protolanguages. Perhaps in the future, words can evolve to a simplified phonetically sound-based language that is more logical like our current music note system or Esperanto. Perhaps it would reveal the primal symbolic communication of God where all letters' symbols are based off of a master shape similar to the carragemother hagel rune. We could then use computers to translate our old illogical writings to see what meanings we might have missed.

Letter symbol, sound and insights~~~*

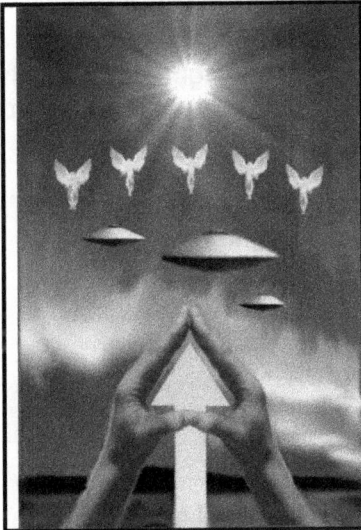

Attention

At the Alter Apex in Air Above the high Arc of the Arrows Arch marks the High Archy of the *Authority* Ascension of All Ancient Alien Anunnaki Angels, Aten, Atman, Amen, Awen, Allah, Auroras.

1

Letter A) At or Above

A is an **Arc**haic+**fact**]Artifact Egyptian glyph of an **A**phis bull head that points **A**t the **A**ir **A**bove apward/upward to the **A**pex. Found in words **A**lpha meaning the beginning of **A**ncient **A**ntiquity. The triangle shape connects two poles at the Apex of a triangle which also contains the symbol of the eye of providence, controlling from **A**bove in the shape of a pyramid representing knowledge, strength and power. Like an **A**rrow of **A**rchery that **A**rches in **A**ir mirrored in movement of the planets above.

The Latin word **A**ster means star of

At+(**S**top+ are/at)**star**+**name**+**see**]Astronomy and Astrology. **A**'s connection with **A**ir suggests that the **A**ir+**ones**]Aryans may have been the **A**nnual+**A**nkh+**key**]Anunnaki or Aanu the Hopi word for **A**nt people of **A**ncient **A**liens and related to the **A**rchetype **high+Arch+see**]hier**A**rchy **A**ll+**ligiture+arch**]oligarchy of the **A**rch+**angels**]Archangels in control the **A**rk/**arch** of the **coven+act**]covenant.

A is also found in **A**uroras and **A**ura of the Earth.

A is found in **A**ncient deities **A**ten, **A**tman, **A**men, **A**wen and **A**mun of the **A**mulet. We give **A**ttend+**shown**]Attention at **A**ten, (the **Sol**/name of **at+StAr**]aster **S**un+**are**]Sol**A**r sun God) which was depicted riding in an **A**rch across the sky going and rowing in

15

his Ark fall+low)flow+boat]float.
When smArt men stArted the Art of Arranging Angles of Arches
they were called Architects and created Artifacts of Archaic
Archaeoastronomy that we find in Stonehenge and pyrAmids.
They also are the (Awe+Thor)Author+write/right+be]Authority
that approve Authors to Archive and carve cartoon like cartouches
At +Light+cenTer+Repeating]Alter.
Where "are" they/"Where art thou"/"Where at thou?
Absolute+(destroy+track)distractions]abstractions enable
abilities to abscond about abnormal absolute abbreviations.
Admit that adhereing to addictive address does not
addition+vocal+make]advocate adventure, it adjourns.
Stay emotionally enamored by this amorous amiable amigo
because I automatically autograph my autobiography with
autonomy.

A functions at the end of words
ad) have+done]had bull+had)bad sorrow+had]sad,
mean+had]mad glee+had]glad etc.
ant/an/act, ake vibration+chant]vibrant, coven+act]covenant.
collect+shown)collection+at+makes]collates,
liberal+at+make]liberates.

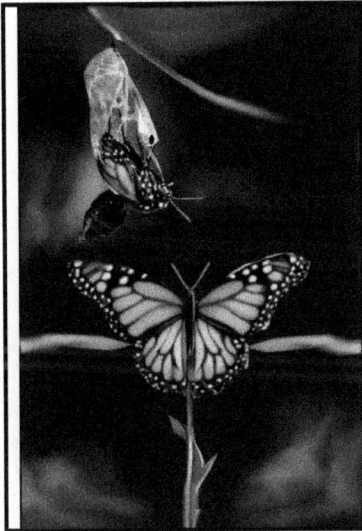

Becoming

is Beginning, Ba Be
Baby is Born, Birth
Bleeding, Bursting,
Being Breathing.
Balance like Ball
Bisected in Both
Brain, Breasts, Butts,
Bottoms, Buttocks,
Bicycles, Bees, Bugs
and Butterflies wings.

2

Letter B) Becoming or Bi

The shape of a **B** in profile looks the lips. In Egypt the word **Ba**
means soul. When a **biota+logos+all]**Biological **Ba-be**/baby, is
Born, it Bursts out, Blooming and Blossoms and is Birthed, and
Becomes Beginning of Being and takes a Breath of invisible air
as soul has enters its **Ba+down+be]**Body.The letter **B** pronounced
is "be" as in "to be or not to be". It is the
Beginning+**cause]**Because of things; that are Below, Beneath
and Basement are where the foundation is found.

Bi The letter **B** is a **B**alanced shape. A single line symbolically
divides **B** into two like A**B**ove/**B**elow or like the wings of **Bi**sected
insects, **B**ugging **B**ugs, **fl**ying+g**littering]**flittering
fluttering+**by]**Butterflies, **bu**sy+di**zzying]**buzzing **B**ees,
busy+**in**+**ess**ence]business of Birds, Bats. It's like our Bulging
Brain, Breasts Bottom/Bum/Butt/Buttocks on Bicycles!
(bisect+**t**ake)**bite+in]**bitten **bi**nd+**are**+thee]binary **bi**sect+**two]**bits,
and bytes are com**mon+bind**ing]combining Bonding.
Balance is good Bountiful, Behaved, The Beneficial Benefactor
Benefits the Beneficiary with a Beautiful **be-not-
violent]**Benevolent benediction.

<u>B+L</u> connects to **bl**ind+l**ack**]black, **bl**ind+w**ink**]blink,
blind+t**eary**]bleary and **bl**ack+h**ue**]blue.

<u>B function near the end of words</u>
<u>ble)ball/bal</u>

See ha**rd+balls**]marbles, **ball+little**]bullets, **up+balls**]apples,
ball+looney]balloons, **bul**ge+**ball)bulb+balls**]Bubbles of
bellowing belches, **scr**aped+j**am**med+**balled**]scrambled eggs
and, ear **low+ball+is**]lobs all have a **glo**be+**ball**]global shapes.
So wear a **bell+t**ight]belt below the big beluga **bell+belly**]belly
when you go to **ball+hole**]bowl.

When the Ballerina stays steady like **ball+last**]ballast, they
(**ball+st**ance)**bal**ance+displ**ay)**]ballet. But when the Ballerina
starts **b**obbin+w**obbling**]bobbling she then forward+**ball**]falls.

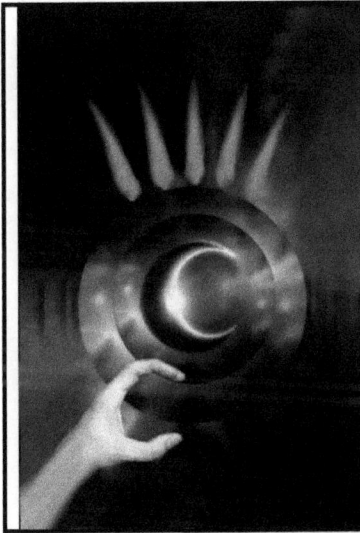

Circling

Cycle Circumstance
Covering Core
Confidence, Controls
Crown Corona of
Consciousness.
Chi Comes whiCh
Changes I Ching
Choice like Chronos's
Challenging Child,
moon Chandra.

3

Letter C)K /S Sound Conscious, Circular or Change

See+peek)seek+right]**secret,** there is no C sound. The letter C
says it's name is Ce/See. C says K or S sound and makes
C+H)chi+range]change.

Discover, uncover hand profile symbol **C** makes a circular shape
swaying+**curve**]swerve seen in **cone**+retained]contained and
turns up in a **sc**rape+(**c**urve+**up**]cup+**soup**]scoop.

Cir]**circular** The letter C also makes an esS S sound, in words
such as circumstances, circulation and the
(**circ**le+**enter**)center+all]central of our **circ**le+**us**]circus.

Con/Kon C makes either a **K** sound in words conjures confidence
congress, controlling, consciousness, crystal, crowns,
corporations, corporals, chiropractors, and chemist.

Cl]**closed** kluged clues, clap, clasp, collapse.

Ch]**change** C+H]Ch sound found in **Ch**inese, **Ch**i, The I **Ch**ing
book of **Ch**ange. The game **Ch**ataraji is a battle of 4 kings of the 4
changing quarter directions. The moons name is **Ch**andra and
changes in phases like ea**ch ch**ild. Sometimes **Ch** makes a Sh
sound as in chivalry or K sound as in **ch**emist and **Ch**rist and
Chronos.

Destruction

Descending Down, to
Dark Dusk Dim Doom,
of Dust, Dirt, Destiny,
Done Demise Death
leads to rebirth.
The Dubious Diabolic
Devolved *Devil*, evil
evening villain
Divides visions with
self-chains of fear.

4

Letter D) Down, Destruction

After reaching its Apex, the letter **D** shape shows the **D**ecending path of the Sun **D**own+**climb**ing]declining in the sky. This **D**ownward motion **cor**rectly+**relates**]correlates to **D**emise, **D**eath, **D**oom, **D**estruction, **D**ust, **D**irt, **D**escend **D**own, and **D**own+evil+ill]**D**evil.

D also reveals an end at the beginning in such words as **D**ictator, **D**ictated, **D**ictionary, and **D**ictation because here, **D**'s influence is that there is finality in authority has **D**ecreed+**sided**]**D**ecided and put some ideas down.

D function near the end of words

<u>ed)</u>di**D**/dea**D**/**D**one Any verb that is already been done is something that you "did" and in a sense is dead. For example; **love**+**d**id]loved, **play**+**d**id]played, **reserve**+**d**id]reserved".

Essence

Early East Electric
Energy is Easter
Eggs Essential Elixir
Effervesce, the
Estrogen Embraces
Eminent Emerging
Emerald Estuaries of
the Earth at the
Equal Equinoxes
over the Equator.
5

Letter E) Energy, Essence

E] Energy+Above+**st**op]East/Estrogen is the Entry point of the Early sunrise Energy on the Earth. The shape of the letter E with its 3 horizontal bars is like sunrays. When the Earth is at an Easterly position to the Sun, there is Equal and Even amount of day light and night at the spring Equinox. This is when the life Energy springs up and is reborn near Easter and the ancient Egyptian Festival Sham el Nessim when they breathed in the **Es**ter+**scent**+all]Essential Effervesces of the fresh oxygen in the air.

E function near the end of words
en)end When something is finished, it reaches the end.
wove+end]woven, **write+en**d]written, **prove+en**d]proven, etc.
ense/ence/ness/is s**ense** of e**ss**ential ess**ense**
cone+(deep+essence)dense]condense t**ight+essence**]tense.
es]does **reprodu**ce+do**es**]reproduces, **make+does**]makes, etc.

Far

BeFore ForeFathers
Found Faith For
Future Forward Final
Fall, Finish of Fate.
Flow like Fleeting,
Flowers, like Fleeing,
Fluffy, Fluttering,
Flying Feathered
Flocks, and Flapping
Flags.

6

Letter F) Far, Future, Flow

F] The letter **F**'s has an association with **F**ormer and
Far+view+sh**ore**]**F**uture movement of time. Find **F**aith in **F**ar **F**ast
Forward **F**inal **F**inish of **F**ate like **F**ormer+**fathers**]**F**orefathers that
came be**F**ore.

F+L]**F**ly it takes on relationships to birds. **F**lowing **F**leeting
Fleeing **F**luffy **FL**ocks of **F**lying **F**lapping **F**eathered birds that
Flew.

FL function near the end of words
Full **Hope+Full**]hopeful **art+full**]artful

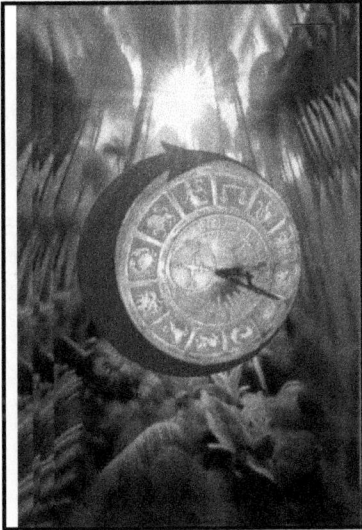

Good

Go Give Great,
Grandmothers Green
Grand, Gold Gift of
Gnostics noticing
Gnosis of Gnomon
shows shadow glow
of now. Ghouls, of
Gravity's Grave are
Gusts of Ghastly,
Ghost spell Gospels.

7

Letter G) Good, Glitter, Great

G makes a **J** sound as in George. or **G** sound as in **GO** and has sometimes been mysteriously paired with a silent **H** and becomes silent when paired with **N.**

The symbol of **G**'s shape is like the left side of a Yin Yang sign with represents the increasing light of the light cycle from the northern hemisphere. The symbol of **G** starts in the center and then progresses as a left sided upward **C**urve like the morning arch of the Sun. **G** can be associated with **G**rowing and **G**ood things like **G**iving, **G**reat, **G**rand, **G**old, **G**ifts.

G+H) as in God+**host**]**G**host and **G**hastly **G**houls. It also associated with **G**oblins, **G**usts, polter**G**eists, and God+**spells**]Gospels.

G+N) has also been deliberately complicated by becoming silent when paired with N. Notice/**G**nosis God+**name+on**]Gnomon disassociates with the word knowledge, although there is a clear relationship.

GL) (glow+over+be)**glory**+find]glorify glow+be)**glee**+had]glad to see the sunbeam's glow+stream]gleam like, queen of the serene good glow+**amorous**]glamorous glow+splendid]Glenda whose glow+flaring]glaring glass+gaze)glaze glow+litters]glitters and glistens galore.

<u>GE)</u> **Gene**+gno**sis**]genesis/ **genes**+of+**Isis**]genesis generated Indian+**genesis**]indigenous.Genitalia generates genetic gender gestated congenital genes and germane germs that will germanate and **re**peat+**generate**]regenerate **gen**e+**era**+make+shown]generations.

<u>GR)</u> Gratified great grey **grand**+mother]Grandma grants con**s**cious+**gratitude**+(**elevate**+make)e**late**+**sh**own]congratulation for g**rad**e+you+make+shown]graduation to **grace**+**show**+**us**)gracious (**great**+full)grateful+**attitude**)gratitude.

Health

Host Hospitality of Hospital is Helps those in Held+ill Hell back to Held+even Heaven. Holy Healing Human well Health wealth. Hips *Hold* & Heave even eaves of Heavy Hipped roof Holy House Habitat.

8

Letter H) Half, Hold, Health

The shape of the letter **H** is a diagram of balance because it is two legs connected in the center like the two hands around **Hole**+did)hold+lift+up]hip and Hold+**elevate**+did]Held **or** Hold+me**ld**]**held** a baby, a **Human**+be]He, Human+**is**]His and Human+repeat**er**]Her of our Herd of Heredity. This balance idea is validated through the word, **Hold**+**eaves**)Heave+very]Heavy of a House, Hold+**dangle**]Hang and the phrase "Hang in the balance", and Half. It also demonstrates working towards balance in Help+ill/**elevate**)Heal+**theos**]Health+even]Heaven, Holy+ghost)Host+spirit+total)Hospital+it+be)Hospitality+solst**ic e**]Hospice. **H** can symbolically correlate to "even" in the Biblical name for God, YHWH if seen as a representation of the four directions.

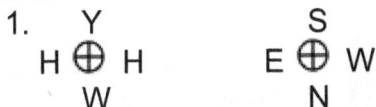

1.　　Y　　　　　　　S
　　H ⊕ H　　　E ⊕ W
　　　W　　　　　　N

In example 1., the Hold+even]Heaven is the times of the spring and fall equinoxes) Half balance equal light and darkness per day. It is the time of year when the Earth crosses over the celestial plane of the Sun and the suns perpendicular rays "pass over" the Earths equator. This ancient H correlation is supported with the Hindu Spring celebration holiday called "Holi," if you take account that their calendar has moved off of the equinox due to the precession of the equinoxes. The name Holi also nicely relates to our Heavenly word Holy+day]Holiday.

Spring and fall Equinoxes are the idea of "even". Even as a description of a time of day is supported by the word "Evening" and twist+light]twilight, as the even light and dark+(even+ill)evil]devil time of the day. Additionally, S+even]seven represents the Sun symbol of two triangles intersected triangles with a dot in the center totalling 7

H function near the end of words
This idea of Hold+even]Heaven as even Half balance is reinforced by (T cross marks the spot ⊕ /T+Heaven]THeta/Theos/God found in words birth, health, death, truth, North, South, month and with.

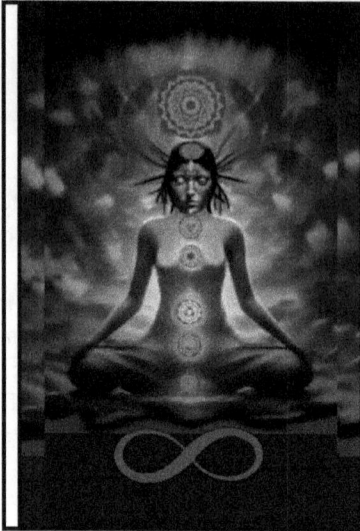

Inner

Infinite sea I see
Inside has no sides.
There In Ides of my
mInd's Iris eye I mine
to find rhymes. I
Lacking light is black
chilling ill of illegal
killing, military,
villains, Illuminati,
Devils vile liabilities.

9

Letter I) Inner

I)ize/is/I/eyes The letter **I** in ides is an inner **dive+ide]**dividing line where we **divide+side]**decIde between two sides, It is the mId mInd midpoint Inside of our body where the two mirrored halves meet and where our line of chakras is located down the middle of our body. It is the line inside us that is the symbol of the letter **I**. When we speak of ourselves, we speak of **I**. Ized added to the end of word can be equated to eyezd/I+eyed/I+did as in the words such as **memor**y+**I**+d**id]**memorized, and **hypnot**ic+**eyes**+**I**+d**id]**hypnotized.

I+N)negative/nothing, this indicates inner, inside found in, inner/inter+**specter+all)spect**acle+**sh**own]introspection with the third eye, or I in your center.

I+LL or lack of light or loss and **ill**ness can lead to death or No/ nothing+il]Nil which means zero or nothing. If you combine pointing Above up/**A**dam and downward pointing **Down+Eve**ning+**ill]**devil. **E**ve, both indicating the two halves of the sun cycle. Many words have **ill** effects such as **ill**usions **ill**egal, **Illumi**nate+**not**+**see]Ill**uminati, military, villain, artillery chilling, killing, **ill**egitimate, **ill**ogical liabilities, libel, debilitating, disabilities. These can lead to **Judge+at+ill]**Jail, h**eld/h**eat+**ill]**Hell.

I function near the end of words.
ian)man/I+am/shown/shn Caucus+man]Caucasian, became
magic+i+am]magician, **physical+I+am]**physician,
politic+i+am]politician and **mortis+i+am]**mortician.

 tion/ion/ish/sh)shown is a contraction of the word
(Shine+how)show+seen]shown is sounds like "shn". Any
verb+**shown]**verbtion becomes a noun, because it becomes
visible and tangible and "shown" Examples:
organize+**shown]**organization, **celebrate+shown]**celebration,
pose+**sit+shown]**position, **At+ten**se+**shown]**Attention,
visible+**shown]**vision, **fin+is+shown]**finish, and
dim+minimize+show+did]diminished.

ing) Any verb+wing)"verbing The hieroglyphic bird
wind+flying]wing symbolized moving motion that evolves into the
suffix "ing". The moving wheel of will is like wind on wing a
repeating wing back and forth round ring of doing like
switch+**wing]**swing/**sw**ay+**wing]**swing, **skat**e+**wing]**skating, and
laugh+wing]laughing.
ism) is+am]ism is revealed in **mystic+is+in]**mystism,
bath+is+am]baptism, **critic+is+am]**criticism, etc
fy/ied)find Seen in **horror+find]**horrified, **special+find]**specify,
quality+find]qualified, **ident**y+**I+find]**identified etc..
ific) i+make]ic Seen in **terror+i+make]**terrific,
monastery+i+make]monastic, **mag+i+make]**magic, and
specify+i+make]specific etc.
ive) i+have]ive Seen in **con**e+**see+I+have]**conceive,
object+I+have]objective, etc.
ize) i+see/eye+see Seen in **sympath**y+**eyes]**sympathize,
critic+eyes]criticize, etc

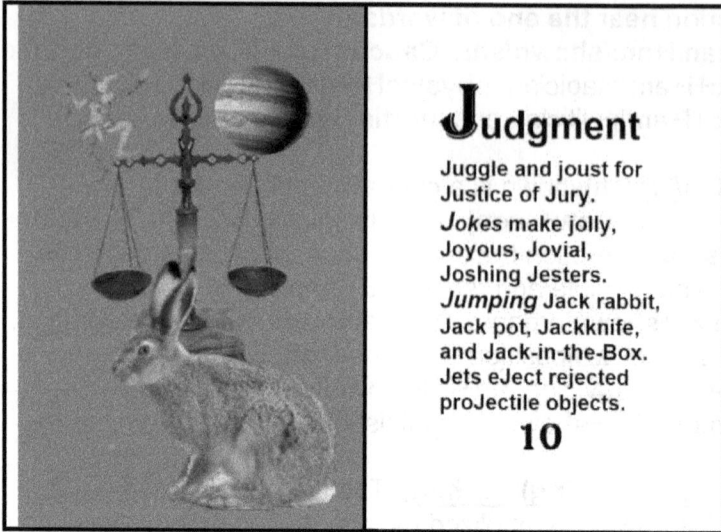

Judgment

Juggle and joust for Justice of Jury.

Jokes make jolly, Joyous, Jovial, Joshing Jesters.

Jumping Jack rabbit, Jack pot, Jackknife, and Jack-in-the-Box. Jets eJect rejected proJectile objects.

10

Letter J) Judge, Joke, Jump

J Judgment Originally, **I** and **J** were different shapes for the same letter. The Judgment of J is found in jury, justice, jousting, Jupiter.

J funny The humor of J is found in joking, jolly, jovial, joy, juggling, joshing, jesters.

J jump The J jump effect is seen in jack rabbit, jack pot, jackboot, jackknife, Jack-in-the-Box and Jack jump over the candlestick. I interject the subject that the **Jets jolt** and eject the rejected projectile objects.

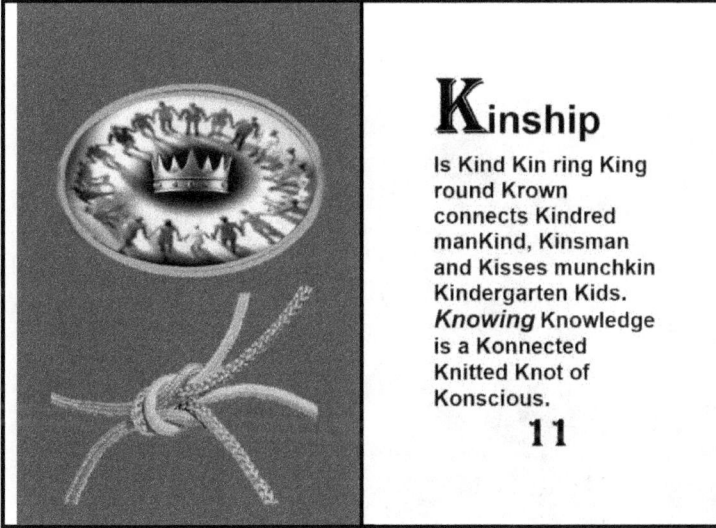

Kinship

Is Kind Kin ring King
round Krown
connects Kindred
manKind, Kinsman
and Kisses munchkin
Kindergarten Kids.
Knowing Knowledge
is a Konnected
Knitted Knot of
Konscious.

11

Letter K) Kinship, Connect, Quest,

The **K** sound sometimes presents as a letter C and represents a hurtful force as in words such as **k**ill, **k**ick, **c**ut, **c**rash, **c**lub, **c**lobber, **c**onquer etc.

K+N The **K** sound when combined with **N** becomes silent in **kn**owing **kn**owledge **kn**itted **kn**ot which have **con**scious+**kn**it+**sh**own]connection like a Key. It is interesting to note that **G+N** the **G** becomes silent like in the word Gnosis. So, this raises the question of why some N sound words have a **G** and some a **K**?

KinshipThe small of man**K**ind are **K**indergarten munch**K**ins **K**ids. Familiar family are **K**ind bump**K**in **K**in, and all **K**insman are in the **K**ingdom of the **K**in+r**ing**]**K**ing who wears the **K**ing+**Round**]Kroun/Crown.

K+W]QU The KW sound is in many words like **Question+is]Qu**iz, **Question+count+it+be]Qu**antity, **Quest+wonder+be]Qu**andary etc., Symbolically the right side of the **K** looks like two choices of a Kw/**quest+sh**own]question pointing above or below, yes or no. Or perhaps it is a glyph for person walking on a quest.

OK Means all/O**ll**+(correlated+right]Correct/Korrect]OK, where O is a **cir**cle+**come**+re**ference**]circumference around **A**bove+**light**]All.

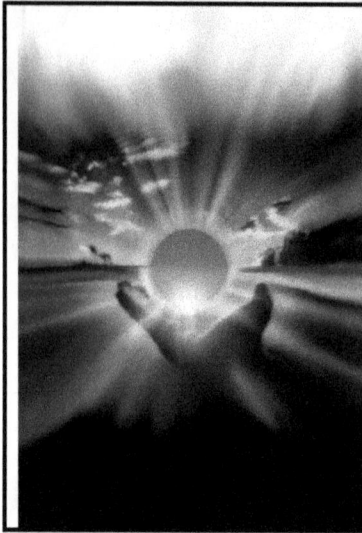

Letter L) Light, Lack

<u>L) Let</u> an enabling quality. Letters Let and Leave us Learn
Literature to Learn+read]Lead. The words lease and lend are
also forms of letting like lift, live, like, life, luck and love.

<u>L Light</u> Light is found in Lux, Luxury, Luxor and Luminance and
illuminate. The name Lucifer was a name for Venus because it
was Luminous. The name Lucy also means Light and Saint
Lucy's day, the 13th of December is when a crown of candles is
worn as a symbol of Light. Long ago Saint Lucy's day fell on the
West+in)wind+inter/inner/enter]winter solstice but moved due to
the procession of the equinoxes before the calendar was reformed
and stabilized.

<u>L Lack</u> also has a negative effect of be+low)below or lack
revealed in words such as late, lost, loss, and lazy.

L function near the end of words

le) is found in pole, hole, point+(dip+hole)dimple]pimple,
bulb+hole]bubble, and top+pole]topple. Hole/hold Is logically
hand+hold]handle, hold+save]have,
at+under+hole]tunnel, ped+hold]pedal, and tablet+hold]table.
less) Seen in many words endings, low+essence]less is found in
priceless, wreckless, worthless, etc.

Magic

Magi, Master, Majesty
Magnanimous Man's
Mind Manipulates
Maps Manifestations
and Manages Material
Matter of Monolithic
Monstrous, Mountain
Monuments with
Much My+need
Money Masonic Mojo.

13

Letter M) Mind, Magi, Man, Myth, Muse, Mono

M) The power of **Me**+(I/**eye**)**My**/**Mi**ne)+find]Mind, a**M** and **my**+**other**]mother.

M+A) Man manipulates manifestations and manages maps and material matter with Magi, Magical, Master, Majesty and Magnanimous (**I'm**+**magi**c+**inner**)**Imagine**+make+**sh**own]imagination.

M+Y/why **Mi**st+**story**]mystery and misty mystical mythical myths.

M+U/under expressed in muse and amusing museum where Muses, make, amusing, music. When the muse is stopped it is (**mu**se+**T**/center)+**dead**]muted.

M Mount+ One/All) mono and monolithic, monogamy monstrous, monumental mountains and money.

M function near the end of words.

Am) Is present tense first-person singular of be. It is found in many words such as: **Sol**+**Above**+**am**]salaam, **Ra**+**am**]Ram, **Above**+(**Down**+**am**)dam]**Adam** of Biblical characters Adam and **Eve**n+**ring**]evening.

No

Nil, Nothing None
Negative Notorious
Naughty Nasty
Noxious Nausea Nag
Need. Not Now.
North gate negate
Nocturnal Cold Dark
hiding hibernation
protects you. Natural
Nice Nurturing Nature

14

Letter N) No, Negative, Nature

N No, Nil, Negative effect because of its
negative+**go**+**l**+m**ake**+**sh**ow**ns**]negotiations association with the
North+aught]naught/ot/ought/zero]not.

K+N) Combined with a **K, N becomes** positive effect in the words
"know and knowledge." Why is KN not applied consistently for
words **N**otice, **N**ote" and "gnosis new, nice, nature, nurture,
natural?

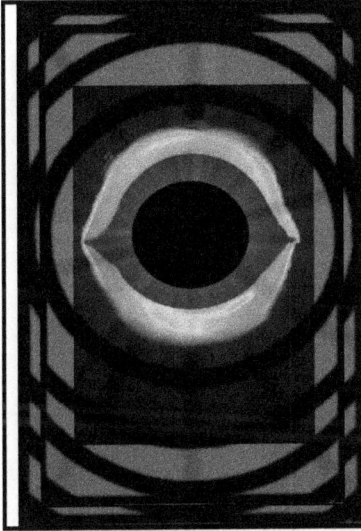

Origin

Oral spOken Open mOuth hOly Om Oll sOund. The Old have been many Orbits arOund One SOn SOl. Orb Outer *Order* all Orrery Of encompassing Omega that leads to Oblivion Obituary.

15

Letter O) All/Oll, Origion, ROund, MOuth

O)all encompassing. It is the Origin beginning and goes around full circle to the ending.

It is the rOund shape that the mOuth makes Open arOund and making the Om hOly sOund.

The Orange is the living symbol of SOl the Sun's sunlight.

Old is One who has been around the wheel of life.

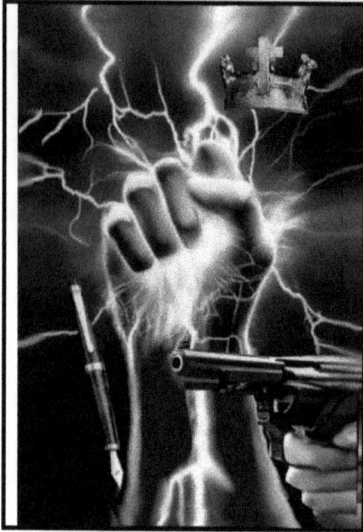

Power

Patriarchy metroPolis
Politician Presidents,
Police, Professors,
Prophets and Popes
Priests *Punish* Pirate
Perpetrators with
Punches, Pointed
Pencils, Pistols, Put
in Penitentiary Pens
of the Penal system.
16

Letter P) Power, Plant, Pi

P power repeating P when **P**rounounced **P**rojects an outward **P**uff force and **P**ower when s**P**oken in s**P**each. The letter symbol shows a line with a **P**rotrusion sticking out from it.

Many **P** words **P**oint out **P**rotrusions such as **P**encils, **P**ole, **P**ins **P**enises that **P**our **P**ee like **P**iss+tool]**P**istols.

P is **P**erpetrators are **P**unch+i+ha**v**e)**P**unitive+d**id**]punished **P**atriarchy's **P**enitentiary **P**ens of the **P**enal system.

Center **P**ole is **P**ower **A**bove+**pole**+**O**/oll/all]A**P**ollo, recognized as a god of light, the sun, and truth. Pole is found in **P**olaris and the north and South **P**ole, and the op**po**sites of **y**es+**point/pole**]yep and **n**o+**point**]nope, **pol**itics, **multi+pole**]multi**ple**, **metro+polic**e]metropolis, and ti**m**e+**pole**]temple.

PL) Power**+l**and**+sp**ace]place planet, plant, plants plots plateaus places to plan to plow. Benevolent effect **pl**ea+**ease**]please, pleasant, plenty, platitude pledges.

P+R) Power+**R**epeating+**t**eacher]preachers projecting, pronouncing, prophets profiting and professors professing and programming **peep**+h**ole**]people, pupils-eyes holes to the brain and are also pupils; pupa students watching and learning.

P+I]pi/3.14 Used to calculate Round circumference and in words for round items: pizelle, pizza, pies, pins, pine cone, pickles, pills, pillar, pipe, pineapple, pierogi, piazza, pixel, pit and "Leaning tower of Pisa".

Quest

Query Question, Quantify, Quiz and Quote Quintessential Quantum answers. *Quiet* Quality Queen essence Quits Quarrels Qualms Quagmires and Quandaries and calmly Quilts.

17

Letter Q) Quest, Choice

Q)question or choice

Qu/Kw. Sounds like **K** and the shape of **K** shows two forces coming together in the middle and finding the answer to a question. A Q shape shows the O of all/OII with a line pointing into the center. The word **Que** in Hindi and Spanish is pronounced **K** and means "what or why/Y" Y is again a symbol of choice. The Q+U could symbolically mean center understanding, or K +W could symbolically mean choice what. Query Quest, and 5th+sense/**Quin+essential**]Quintessential **Q**uestions + **w**hat, **w**here, **w**hen, and **w**hy.

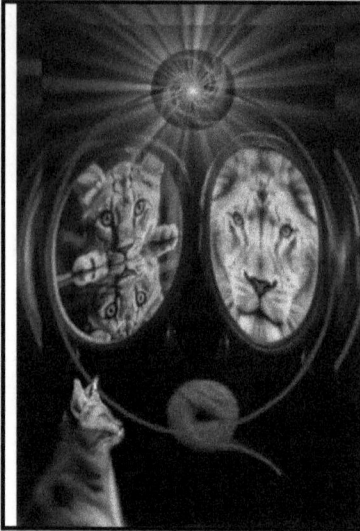

Reflect

Red Ruby Ra Rays
Radiate in Radiant
Radius, Roll and
Revolve in Round
Ring of puRRing
RoaRing *Repeating*
Reeling, Revealing
Returns Real Revered
Rainbow Reason
Rhythm Rhyme.

18

Letter R) Round Repeating

Ra/Egyptian name for the Sun found in
auspicious+**ro**ar+**Ra**]Auro**Ra** and **Ra+in+bow**]rainbow. Many
Rulers+cl**aim**)**R**eign to be descended from the Sun. Could
Ra+far+elevated]**R**afael, **R**ama, **R**amses, **R**aja, **R**asta also be
derived from **Ra**?

er/re/repeats The symbol shape of the capital **R** symbolically
looks like a **R**ound ball circle walking with two legs, and rolls on
the tounge when pronounced. The **R+sound**]round of ring of
singing is a round. **R** adds a **R**epeating effect at the beginning and
end of words such as **R**epeate**R**, **R**evolve**R**, pu**RR** that are
Redoing **R**ing action like a **R**evolving door cycle. When One
Repeatedly **do**es+wing/r**ing**]doing action, they
Are+at)**Art+re**peat]**A**Re a **do+roll**]doe**R**/ **Do+R**epeat]doe**R**. The
ci**R**cle/cycle/chak**R**a is a **R**ound cycle symbol like the Horus/
hours on a clock face. Hou**R**s represents **R**ays/**R**epeating on
Sun/**Hor**us+ri**se+son**]Horizon.

Ho**R**us ci**R**cles like a Oraborus to**R**us **R**epeating Winte**R** and
Summe**R**. In the word Mi**RR**o**R,** mir means water the double **R** is
Repeated **R**eflection of **Ra**. **He+R**eproducer]he**R** is a female.

Letter S) See, Show, Sign

The letter S is related to the Sun and the South and is found in the (In and Above) y**I**n y**A**ng symbol. When you look at a compass with the S or South at the top and imagine an O in the circle middle with the N at the bottom, it spells the word SON? Additionally, look at the relationship to the word SIN which was the Babylonian word for Moon.

South	**S**outh
Outter	**I**nner
North	**N**orth or Nil equating = 0 position on the compass
Sun	Moon
Light	Dark
On	In

Sin became associated with inner darkness and things Negative. Perhaps the idea of vast infinite dark inner world inside was fearful to primitive people because it could include nightmare dreams or **sin**ister imaginings that drove people to do evil acts or insanity.

The **S/s**hape in the center of the circle O of the yin yang symbol is created by movement of the Chi or energy that changes direction

at the Solstices. In the Southern hemisphere, if one places a
STake in the ground, and then starting on the summer sols**ST**ce,
plots the shadow length every fifteen days around the outside of a
circle inward until the **West+in)**wind+**inter/**inner/enter]winter
solstice. Then after the chi energy changes direction, the shadow
lenght is then plotted from the center of the circle outward. So, the
S is related to the Sun ray energy. The Saint Lucia buns made on
St Lucy's day in December are shaped like an **S**.
S+One)Son+hole**Soul/Sol+un**der]Sun. Is it a coincidence that
these words are related by sound and similar meanings? Do they
have a primitive historic relationship?

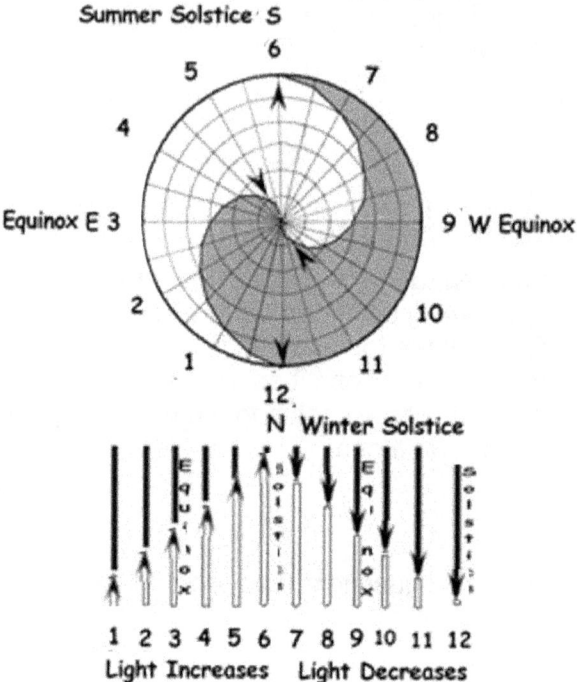

Summer Solstice S

Equinox E 3

9 W Equinox

N Winter Solstice

1 2 3 4 5 6 7 8 9 10 11 12
Light Increases   Light Decreases

Shadow lenght dependant
upon Latitude

S+T Stop S/Sun/Sol+T/cross]St+oppose]**stop** is in **st**art, **st**ill,
stall, **st**ay, **st**uck, **st**unned, **st**able, **st**op of Winter and Summer

Sol+stop+i+see+cease]SolSTices and Early+stop]EaST+turn]Eastern term and wet+stop]west+turn]western term. Perhaps sticks or stave+half]staff, stick+make]stake-out, stud, stem, and indicate the stop spot. The stop effect also makes sense in stifle, stop+hammer]stammer, stalemate, stop+glare]stare, statue, and state.

S+T+R
(Stop+Repeating+pain]strain+long)strong+length]strength+l+have)strive, fraught+strain+make]frustrate, inner+structure]instruct, straight+edict]strict, strai,ght+meet]street, and strain+angle)strangle+choke]stroke.

S+P To Say+Put+it]spit+utter]sputter with a spiraling spin+hold]spindle, spin+done]spun, spin+at]spit motion that relates to our mouth like a speak+reach]speech and speak+tell]spells. Similar words include, spoon, speech, speak, spray, sprinkling, springs, spurt, spout and spring+out]sprout.

S+L Slow+soft]sloth slope+crouch]slouch couch and slide+lump]slump, slide+under]slumber steep slide+deep]sleep (slope+ride)slide+low]slow, slide+lay]sleigh and (slip+guide)slide+bed]sled
S+N Slide+make)snake+seek]sneak snake+viper]snipes+catches]snatches snacks. Snooty snoopy snobs' snub, sneer, snicker and snout snores, snorkles, sniffs, sneezes snot.
S+H Shamash/Shamesh+man]Shaman sees Om Shanti sun shine+seen]sheen and (shine+made)shade+(shine+know)shows]shadows.
S+W Swinging+lay)sway+wiggle]swiggle swine+handle]swindle etc.

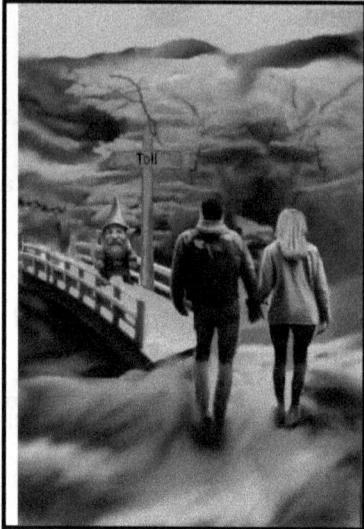

Truth

Is Two Twisted and interTwined like Twirled lights of Theos' Twilight. Trek and Tread the Track to Travail and Trounce Thru and *Transfer* a-cross the Terrestrial Trolls' Terrible Tariffs.

20

Letter T) Truth, Cross

A+T/cross in the cenTer of a circle is a symbol for the Earth ⊕ It is also an archaic symbol of theta ⊕ which is found in enTHusiasm and **TH**eos which means God/aT+Hermetic. **Theos+at)that+is]**this.

It is also a symbolic representation of the sun is in the center circle of orbit of the earth. The four points are the two solstices and two equinoxes.This is perhaps why "NorTH, SouTH, EarTH, long+to+hold]lengTH and **wide+to+hold}widTH moon+th]monTH** and numbers positions fourTH, fifTH etc., end in **TH** because they are markers for celestial turning points.

This idea of **H** as balance works nicely in the nameTHoTH/ Hermes Trimegatis which is the ancient Egyptian God of letters and writing. In antiquity a Herme was a small statue that marked boundary of a border. In this case the **TH** boundary in the word north and South marks the division of light increasing or decreasing in the yearly cycle.

	S		SouTH			H	
E	O	W=	East	**O**	West = yEs	**Wet** = YHWH	
	N		NorTH			H	

The basis of Thought in the middle mind. **TH**ink+**O**/0/ought all/outter/nothing+**Thought**]TH⊕TH is the universe within. Thought is done in the **M**y+Id+n**D**]mind in the I between the two **H**alves of the self. Many words with **O** reveal the cen⊕er is the holy unseen criss-cross of the wheel O/⊕
T/**+**/at/cross+**R**epeat+**U**nder+**Th**eta/God/Balance/Time/]truth ⊕ like a **w**hy+**At**+Chi/**ch**ange]watch face or gnomon.

T+R) Travel see chapter Travel and Carry

T+W) two
T/theta+**w**est is used in the words **two**, **tw**in, **tw**isted, **tw**irled+**lights**]twilight, half light and half dark. All directions contain the **T**/cross in the circle+**enter**]cen**T**er.
Energy+**At**+**st**op]Ea**ST** and **wet**+**st**op]we**ST** the S is a symbol of Sun over/**X** the equator at the equino**x**.
The **ST** in the word fir**ST** may mean faste**ST**, farthe**ST** position.

T function near the end of words
T+A]At Where **T**/**+**/cross/marks a **T**on/town **little+town**]Littleton **farming+town**]Farmington.

Letter U) Unique, Up, Under

Letters U, V and W are related because they point downward and possibly why they are close in the alphabet. W is pronounced "double U", but is written like a double V. Some people pronounce W as V.

U can sound like the word you and is associated with number 1 as in Universe, and unique.

U can also make the sound of A as in under.

The shape of U is a C of circle turned up like a **C**urve+**up**]cUp and indicates **U+n**o+**d**own]under like,

be+low)**be**low+under**neath**]beneath Earth like Austrailia. When the ancients heard a loud boom they said it was

Thor+**under**]thunder. When they

See+(**un**+**d**own+**re**peat)**un**der]Sun **set**, they said it was defeated by the Egyptian God "**Set**" and was

subducted+**merged**]submerged under the Earth.

The **U** under effect is seen in

Mud+(**pit**+**mud**+ho**le**)p**uddle**]muddle,

gouge+(**rut**+**re**peat)ru**dder**]gutter is **rout**e+**in**]routine root to

42

where the **under+taker**]undertaker takes you under. Lke the
bottom half of a circle or or an **umbra+elevated+Above**]umbrella.
UMP **U**p+**m**ount+**p**rojection/pile]**U+MP** creates an
upward/"**ump**ward" arch as in **j**ack+**ump**]jump, **h**ill+**ump**]hump,
bulge+**ump**]bump, **d**own+l**ump**]dump the **c**lod+d**ump**]clump
h**ump**+(**p**ower+**mid**)**pyr**amid]umpire and
plenty+(**p**ush+**up**)**pump**]plump.

U function near the end of words
ure functions like ye**s**+**U**+**are**)sure. Seen in
create+**sure**]creature, con**struct**+s**ure**]structure,
close+(**s**hown+se**cure**)s**ure**]closure, etc.

Victory

Vicious Violent Vile
Volatile Villian
Vandals were Valiant
Vikings of Valhalla.
They deVoured Vital
Valuable Vitamins.
Violated *Victims* were
Virtuous Vixen Vestal
Veiled Virgin goddess
of loVe grooVe.

22

Letter V) Victor, Woman

V is like two up raised arms indicating Victory. The Viking word for
heaven Valhalla, may have related to valiant, victory and value or
Vital words' vitamin, love and live. It is **inter+resting**]interesting
to note that the word "ove" sounds like "of" This makes "I love
you", into "I of you" meaning we are one. It is also found in above
and over.
Another meaning of **V** can be seen in the graphic symbol of the
heart. The upper arches of the heart shape are like round breasts

43

and the lower **V** of a heart matches the shape of the **V**agina groo**V**e of a woman/**V**oman, e**V**e and logically related words', **V**ulva, **V**estal **V**irgin and lo**V**e goddess **V**enus. Is it just a coincidence that **V**enus rhymes with **P**ushing **P**enis? Additional evidence of **V** as a pointing down groove can be found as in the words dive+rivet]divit, divert, grove, groove, cave, cavern and valley.

V also has a connection to **W** which is a double **V**. In some languages **W** is pronounced **V**. A **v**esper is an evening prayer said when the Sun sets in the west. When vesper is said with the **W** sound, it sounds like the word whisper. The word **W**in and **W**on can also be seen to illustrate a victorious/**W**ictorious stance with arms held high in **V**ictory/**W**ictory.

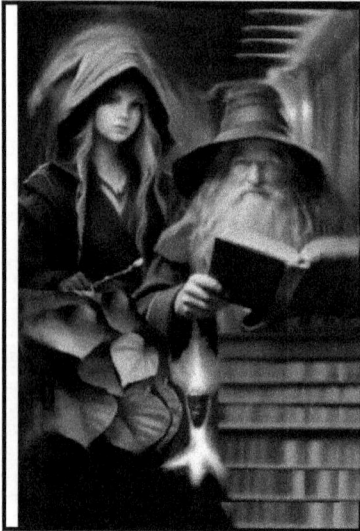

Wisdom

Watch
Wonder+at what,
Wonder+there Where,
Wonder+end when
Wonder+I Why is
the Wisdom *Vision* of
Wise+herd Wizards
and Witty Wishing
Whispers, Which is of
Wit+change Witches.

23

Letter W/Wh) Wonder, Question Wise Wit Wizards

H
Y⊕ W
H

S
E ⊕ W
N

W is found in YHWH, which could symbolic representation of the four directions. **Y**/energy East and **W**/West weather. Ancient man surely noticed after the fall equinox that there was less day light when nature took rest when wet weather came from the West and winter winds until Winter Solstice.

W also relates when people have made it around the wheel of life past the rest in the West and descend into the winter end of their lives and become wi**de**+si**ze**]wize with knowledge. The **W** can be seen as making the shape of two arms stretched out with the head in the middle meaning wide. The wide knowledge of questions of **w**ho. **w**hat, **w**here, **w**hen and **w**hy is the **w**it of the **w**itch visualizer, visa**r** wi**se**+he**ard**]**w**izard.

.

See /vid/vis/vit/wit witty

Wise+he**ard**)wizard/**wise**+**ares**)wizards/**wise**+**orate**+di**d**)**words**]w izards/(**why**+**is**)**wiz**+**see**+**words**]wizards have (**Wh**+**Y**)**Wh**y+**eyes**]whys/ wi**se**+**dome**]wisdom. They are whys guys/wise guys, of old odd Oz that tell tales of s**t**ore+sh**ow**)s**t**ow+**orate**+se**es**]stories. They are venerated visionary, **su**per+**pre**mire]supreme, **super**ior+(**advice**+(**vis**ion+**seer**)vizier)ad**visor**]supervisers with valid valuable vigilant vital vivid
li**ve**+**able**)viable invisible visions. They ad**vance**+**vis**ible+**guide**]advise to revise arrive revive to vibrant alive **Sun**+**Arise**]Sunrise.

They In**quire**+**test**/**essence**)**quest**+**shown**]question. Wizards' recognize **real**+**eyes**]realize **real**+**it**+**be**]real**ity** is relative revealed **nature**+**real**]natural and **ether**+**real**]ethereal is **real**+**be**]really/**real**+**lay**]really su**rya**+**real**]surreal **real**+**home**]realm. They In**ner**+**spire**]inspire s**pun**+**in**)s**pin**+**higher**)**spire**+**all**)**spir**als+**it**]spirit to **at**+(**spin**+**higher**)**spire**]aspire up the chakra spine vibe of the tribe.

Wizards and dunces wear **cone**+**all**)**con**ical+(**see**+**inner**)**center**+**make**)**concentrate**+**shown**] concentration hats that **cone**+**dense**]condense

cone+solid+make]consolidate
cone+(circle+enter)center+make]concentric
conscious+essence]consciousness . Like a
focal+cone+us]focus/hocus pocus continually on
conscious+text]context of tenets of conscious+intent]content
makes us competent and confident.
What+yonder]wonder/whonder+Y]Why/Y and Axe+quest]ask
question, leads to a+swear]answer, cause reason. It is no
axe+i+dent]accident that it cuts middle like symbol Y/why and
determines+sides]decides, No or Y+essence]Yes
see+essence]sense evident evidence.
Axe+(sacking+one)Saxon)+make]assassinate take+axe]tax
at+axe]attack, hijack, ram+sack]ransack,
with+(hit+axe)hack]whack and hack+it]hatchet it.
What+how]wow, now+here]near, why+here]where/
wonder+here]where no+where]nowhere questions.
Why+at)what+(head+ear+did)heard]*wheard*/word, of
light+(with+order)word]Lord, in the whO+hole]whOle hOly hOle
sOul. Wonder+end]when, which+you]who, which+human]whom,
wonder+I+choice]which, swap+which]switch.
With+it)wit+change]witch/ Why+it+choice]witch/
wit+wish]witch+choose+be]witchy washy wishy+change]which
they what+change]watch is witch+craft]witchcraft.
Spoken+tells]spells fly like aircraft and are broadcast in the vary
various+able]variable area air. Witness, withered weathered
Wiccan is not wicked aim+bitch+i+is]ambitious wenches
bad+witch]bitches. They have written bewitching worthy
whish+vesper]whispered words of worship late/latter+stop]last
stop in the west til towards see+peace]cease of death rest. Even
Holy soul's holiday is the bewitched
hallowed+(two+between)tween]Halloween. It's not just black
bats, cats and rats trapped by bad rap scene with allegorical gory
gorgeous gourds of hellish hollow Horror+between]Horrorween,
Horror-o-teen.

Letter X) MiX, Intersection

Letter **X** which was the letter Chi, pronounced Ki and this C-H-R combination is found in words relating to Christ, Christmas Chronos, Chromatic. The X symbol sometimes replaces the word in the word Christ and makes Xmas.

X marks the spot and is an important turning point.

In the case of siX, the **X** actually has a line coming straight through the center so it would be more of the asterisk/X symbol with six points.

X also relates to the cross bones and things taboo booze XXX or like a seXy XXX porn movie.

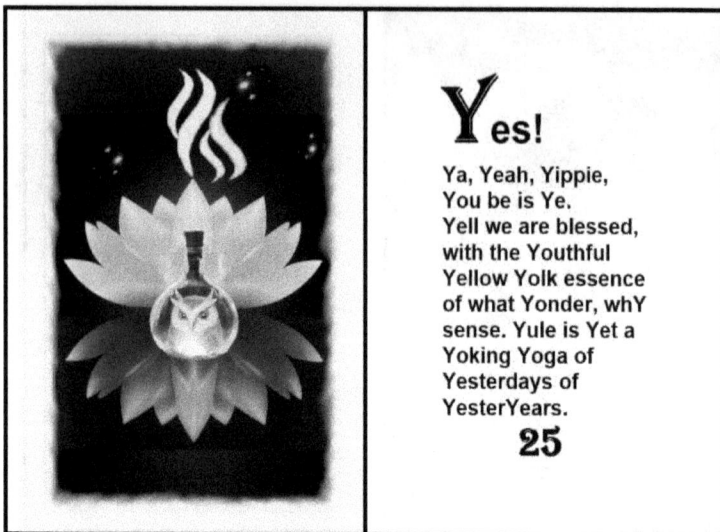

Y es!

Ya, Yeah, Yippie,
You be is Ye.
Yell we are blessed,
with the Youthful
Yellow Yolk essence
of what Yonder, whY
sense. Yule is Yet a
Yoking Yoga of
Yesterdays of
YesterYears.

25

Letter Y) Yes, Why

Y is positive in yeah, ya, **y+es**sence]yes and
Judge+**ess**ence+**us**]Jesus.
This would align with the ancient Babylon name of GoD YHWH.

Yessense

Hold ⊕ H even

W inter

Y is in the position of the Southern direction.
Y also has a relationship to T or theta as revealed in old English
pub signs such as Ye Old Inn which we now write as "The Old
Inn". The W is in the North position.
Y sounds like **WH+I**]why" and looks like question because it is a
vertical line is the question of the topped with two different angle
answers. This is similar to K on its side as a Kwestion with two
outcomes.

Y function near the end of words

<u>ly/ty/y/ like be/to be/see/thee</u> Y found at the end of the words
and means to be. Seen in words **fun+be/see/thee**]funny,
obedient+like+be]obediently, and **novel+to+be**]novelty etc.

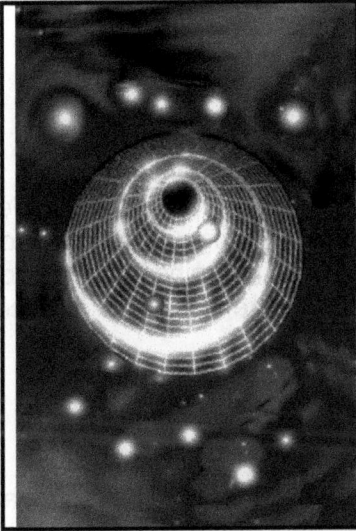

Z en

A to Z All Zooms with Zeal to Zillions at Zenith then in Zephyrs Zaps Zips Zig Zags back in Zen ends Zone to Zilch Zero, snooZing ZZZZzzzz at Zeptepi, then Awakes Zygote to A to Z again.

26

Letter Z) Zen, End

All+Zilch/zero/nothing)A to Z. When something ends/endZ". It means dead as in Zomb+be]Zombie and back to Zeptepi the . first time or the golden age of alchemy where Egyptian gods created reality. So, no thing becomes something and lives.

Hidden Power Card Game A to Z
Available on Ebay

```
                O
      K <on C
      M
      AP
      S<onL
G<B<E< (T<on I <on X <on H) <Y> W>D>F>Q
  J      N                          J
         V
         U
         Z
         R
```

Word Relationships by Subject

I **comm**unicate+**ment**al)comment **mean**+at]meant
cone+**dense**]condensed words **pro**be+**able**]probable, possible
ancient **evol**ved+**solutions**]evolutions, I arrange paragraphs to
relate logically according to subject, word meanings and sound.
But I invite all readers to try to rearrange the words and to decode
other logical kluged words.

Words about Words and Song

Be present with **pre**vious+**sence**]presence for this present of a
present+m**ak**e+**shown**]presentation and **let**+**earn**]learn word
add+**it**+**sh**own]addition. Read the **writ**ing+**end**]written
scribe+dri**bble**)**scr**ibbles+sl**ashed**]scratched derivative ABC's on
in+**not**+**del**ete+**able**]indelible **scr**ibbled+**roll**ed]scrolls and see
they are **di**scovered+**cipher**]deciphered. They
discuss+scribe)**des**cribe+in**scription**s]descriptions and
description+defici**encies**]discrepancies that decide inscribed
transferred+in**scription**s]transcriptions of
manual+**scripts**]manuscripts.
Prevention+(**scri**bble+cry**pt**ic)**script**+**sh**own]perscriptions
depicted picturesque **scr**ibble+**pictures**]scriptures and
portrait+**all**]portrals of **pre**vious+**dict**ated+**shown**]predictions.

Sanitary+**eyes**+**did**]sanitized sane, not tainted saints
sanctuary+harmon**y**+**us**+**see**]sanctimoniously sang forsaken
sacred+**of**+**sanct**uary]sacrosanct
conscious+**secr**et+**make**]consecrated **sac**rifice+**red**]sacred
sanctuary+**writ**ten]Sanskrit songs, sonatas and sonnets. They
repeat+**son**orant+**make**]resonate like **son**ic+**far**]sonar and
soft+sm**oothing**]soothing salaam **s**ongs+**calm**]psalm sagas with
control+in**sist**+**stan**ce]consistant
constant+**son**ic+**stan**ce]consonance
conscious+**son**ic+**stan**ce]consonants with cadence and circling
tingling sounds of
sound+(r**ound**+d**inging**)r**inging**)**s**inging+**long**]songs.

A+maze+doing]amazing
a+(make+use)muse)amuse)+magic)music)+i+am]musician that transmutes and unmutes a museum of timed
meter+sure+did]measured meter+gnomon]metronome similar+metric+all]symmetrical like
a+(writh+drum]rhythm+metric]arithmetic with crescendo crashing+rests]crests. They also
meld/melt+low)mellow+and+holy]melancholy
melt+low)mellow+dramatic]melodramatic melodies of flow+lutes]flutes, and tunes of tonal+hoots]toots of trumpets and
in+(strum+ring)string+hum)strum)+acts)instruments+mental]in strumentals. The Brahmans channeled
in+chanting)enchanting+shown]incantations and chanted+harmony+doing]charming hymns, harmonious humming harmonica and harmonium harmonies with no
hurt+armed]harmed dramatic+harmony+karma]dharma.

They are combined+order+made+did]coordinated with chords+us]chorus and
correlated+stereo+graphed]choreographed choir, and serene+made]serenade like a serious serve+man]sermon serve+us]service of
serene+raphsody+is)Serapis+elohim]seraphim increasing serene+tone+in]serotonin and sure+seen+it+be]serenity.
It is communicates+posed]composed of the prose+hypnotized]proselytized
((prosody+odes)prose+fate)prophet)+poetic]prophetic. (Profess+repeater)professor+i+shown+all]professionals prose+announce]pronounce, proofs and proceed to prove problems proved+found]profound and is a profess+it]prophet of prosaic proposed+found+see]prophesy/
prophet+sees]prophesies through alliterated Poe+rhyme]poems. Protect (Ap/up+prove)approve+all]approval of proceed+to+agony+is]protagonist who provides prose+claim+make+shown]proclamations
problems+feign]profane and proceeds past profuse produced profitable programmed programs of past.

Come+apprehend]comprehend
common+pair)compare+like+rail]parallel parts. Find

quality+find]qualified Aquarian
acquired+quaint+stances]acquaintances, who quasi
question+is]quiz, and don't quiet+like]quite to quit+why+it]quiet.
They quickly (quip+wrote)quote+nip]quip quality+trains]quatrains
notes "so move+rote]mote it be".

Inject+essense]Ingest and taste+essence]test,
gut+estimate]guess essence+make]estimate
query+essence)quest)+shown)question+is]quiz.
What/Quid/Que/est)Key/qui/est) K/question+
Energy+lift]elevate+why/Y/E]Kelly/?+Energy+elevate+why]Kelly

Hold a question+forum]quorum for question+hearing]queries and
in+question+mire]inquires into qualms and
quantity+found+vary]quandaries, question+war+tangle]quarrels,
and question+drag+mire]quagmires.
See the question+slew]queues of quintessential quantum
quantified quality close+cues]clues and find
conquer+quest]conquest key does lay in
see+peek)seek+right)secret)+quest+there+did]sequestered
yesterday.

I seek+(go+to)got]sought, and I
bring+(buy+(go+to)got)bought]brought and
give+lift)gift+have]gave, so you forget+give]forgive, relented
loan, that was lend+let]lent.
If they+lift/left]theft, miss+taken]mistake and
steal+wealth]stealth then they+leave]thief or they+evils]thieves.

Listen, the (liberty+all)liberal+literary]library's
literary+feature]literature letter+really]literally
liberal+make]liberates allegorical and
all+letter+make+shown]alliteration logical logos. Like leading
lattice ladder lyric letters let us
look+earn)learn+sinc)link+guess+mystic)linguistic+usage]langu
age. The theos+ought)thought+link)think to long+stop]lost
logos+make]logic of
ill+(letter+rate+sure)literature+made]illiterate
longing+hang+you+showing]languishing words logged and
locked in legal+it+made]legitimate legible legacy. But
writing/writhing+in)rhythm+time]rhymes prose shows
all+legend]alleged lead lend lift lofty lantern

inner+**lighting**]enlighting **no**+**light**]night sight with
ex**t**ra+in**citing**]exciting inner+**sights**]insights of
lang**u**age+**myth**+mathemat**ics**]langmythics.

A+**sw**orn+h**ear**)**swear**]answer is like **sw**ing+w**iping**]swiping
swishing sweeping switched cutting **swear**+**word**]sword.

Dissing **dis**gusting+**cuss**+**shown**]discussion causes
con**s**cious+**cuss**+**sh**own]concussion percussion.
Cusses+ver**se**]curses are inverted adverse
pervert+ver**se**]perverse reverse verses that convert and
transverse the un**i**ty+**verse**]universe of
reveal+re**late**+**shown**]revelation.
Conscious+**vers**e+**say**+**shown**]conversation are reverberation **of**
ver**b**+**boast**]verbose verbatum and a**dd**+**verbs**]adverbs with
va**l**iant+**true**)**value**+**able**)valuable (**ver**ily+**true**)**virtue**+**us**]virtuous
very variable (**vibe**+**rate**)vibrate+**shown**)**vibr**ation)+ch**ant**]vibrant
verses. With volition and volume we voluntarily
voice+**call**+**i**+**is**]vocalizes **vocal**+**you**+dictio**nary**]vocabulary
vow+**ele**vate]vowels from the void.
Dictionaries dictator's **dictat**e+**shown**]dictations of edicts is no
control+ad**versarial**)**contro**versial+**dictions**]contradictions with
fa**ll**+**see**+**be**]falsely as fact+**make**]fake, fooling/<u>phooling</u>
phoney/foney photos and non-phonetic/fonetic
ficticious+**shown**]fictions or predictions.
But yu nu thru and thru, it twznt tru tu du!
But you knew through and through, it wasn't true to do.

Mistake+**spellings**]mispellings feign far farce fake facsimiles of
fab+**brick**+made]fabricated defaced **fable**+**nebu**lous]fabulous
manu**al**+**facto**ry+d**id**}manufactured perfect **flat**+**story**]flattery fibs,
results in vaulting **summit**+**re**peat+as**saulting**]summer-saulting
fault+**after**]faltering, insults and
(fall+**ail**/fail+**all**)fall+**low**)fallows+**hollow**]follow into
guile+**be**]guilty guilitine into the (**get**+**lull**)**gull**+**able**]gullible hollar
gully+**hutch**]gulch.

Thought+tinker]thinker keeps twist+seeking]tweaking linear
line+connect)link+quest+make]linguistic linkages and
syncronistic+links]syncs words.

Spin yarns tall talk+trail]tell/talk+tell]tale
consciously+knitted]connected net+stick]nest weaves web of
woven+orate+did]words of stow+orate+sees]stories.

The shastra sutras
knit+thought)knot+show)know+alleged]knowledge like a surging
surger and sure+urge)surge+on]surgeon sews sutures.

Allow the allusive all see eye, all-lumination of
illumination+not+see]illuminati to see Alphanumeric Alphabet
from A/Alpha/All to Z/zilch/zer0/0 of 0mit om+mega]omega
and(U/V)(V/W) and Y+E and (K/C)(C/S) C+H relations.

Are these correct+responding]corresponding word
correct+relation]correlations of
able+brief+deviations]abbreviations merely a
common+incidence]coincidence? Perhaps what
happens+hazzardly]haphazardly is
per+(chi/change+advance)chance]perchance
happy+stance]happenstance wrapped in
circle+stance]circumstance.

This collect+show+one)collection+makes]collates,
recall+collection]recollections of letter reflections of
frequent+sequence]frequencies that show theory of
fractured+(fact+actual)factual]fractal refracted
fractured+rag+remnants]fragments. It finds fragile+fail]frail
fray+crack+sure)fracture+all)fractal+shown]fractions and
art+official)artificial+fact]artifact factors actions of attractive
accurate acute cute abstract diffractions that are refracted and
reflected.

Truth+sayer]soothsayer includes not+cultured+truth]uncouth miss+constructed+glued]misconstrued closed+glued]kluge of conscious+kluge+shown]conclusions that previous+conclude]preclude or exit+kluged]excluded due to dubious prove+of]proofs.

But the sleuth accuses, argues pursues a thorough review of a question+(slop+loose)slue]queue of fused issues of kluged cued clues that glue.

So respond+sensibly]responsibly and sponsor respectably. Allude to the collide+shown]collisions in couple+(in+closed+shown)inclusion]collusions.

I confess+hide]confide/conscious+fidelity]confide, conclude+profess]confess, I intend no contentious none+sense]nonsense! Don't down+send]descend to conscious+damn]condemn.

I only cause+shown]caution of cause+make+shown]causations and occasion+current]occurences. I control+victum]convict not+victim+able]invincible to control+vindicate]convince with concrete conversation. A contagion that conscious+inverts]converts consciousness. They conjure conscious+evidence]confidence that conveniently fools. They continue+stand]constant irresistible repeat+insistant]resistant, persevere+insist]persistent, continue+insist+stand]consistent conscious+reserve)conserve+i+have]conservative precious+reserve]preserve nerve.

It is Intended tenacious tensile (in+near)inner+tense]intense out+there]outer tension of consious+tentant]content. So give attention to concentrate+tense+shown]contention and the minds detain+(at+tension)attention]detention.

Can you (conscious+knit)connect+jump+relate]conjugate the cause connotations of continue+tag+us]contagious conscious+scientist+of+us]conscientious cosmic consciousness, and continued+rules]controls?

Complacent complementing compliance is
compilant+illicit]complicit with complete
compete+it+shown]competition
common+promising]compromising complicated complex
company+pact]compact to at+common+make]accommodate.
So, extra+speed+it]expedite don't imped.
Up+scene+bend]ascend, blend, comprehend or
extra+spend+i+have)expensively spend, attend, extend,
be+friend)befriend friend+bond+be)fondly and
repeat+commend)recommend.

Come send calm, content,
comments+mend)commend+make+shown]commendations or
suspence+end]suspend extensive intense dense, tense
consciously+descend]condescending or pretentiously
previous+intend]pretend pretty+tense]pretenses. For in the
impending end, I do not depend on or intend to defend in
response to what you send.

Study Above Attributes

Don't stay still static standing in stub+born]stubborn stances, like
screw+stooges]scrooges. Don't be stop+run]stunned and
stop+runt]stunted in stop+droop)stoop+eye+did]stupefied in
stooped+id]stupid stupor stuck+age]stage. Astute
study+mental]students are understudies who stay+land]stand
under and under+study+stand]understand sagacious
say+age]sages on the stadium stages. Seek sayings of Buddha at
the stupendous steepled Stupa. Study sadhu's smooth soothing
shastra sutured sutras and suitable soothsayer Zarathustra.
Shower with Shakti's and Shiva's shastras. Or tune into the
rotating torus torque of torrential roaring tornado of the tarot and
the torch+Ra]Torah.

We are deteriorated and torn+mental]tormented by
torture+horrid]torrid tore+shown]torsion of the perturbing turning
turbulent turbine of turmoil. So, study stare at static stalactite's

stalagmite status statues and stout stele standing Stonehenge
that still stands in state with stature. Then start, **st**op+gl**are**]stare,
take the **st**op+**up**)**st**ep+ch**air**]stairs straight past Mars to
stellar+**far**]stars

 A**ll**+correct]OK? **Ab**ove+**see**]observe
object+i+ha**ve**)**obj**ective+**ess**ence]obsess over
obscured obvious **obj**ect+**stac**k+ho**les**]obstacles of
object+**struct**ure)**obstruct**+**shown**+is]obstructions.

Ordinary h**Ole**+**pen**]open black hole, and octave of
h**oly**+**Om**]home omen offers organized order, orienting to the
r**otor**+**make**)**rota**te+**making**]rotating core orb orrery
origin+**all**]original aboriginal o**round**+**it**)**orbit**+**torus**]oraborus and
above+**authority**+**of**+**Ra**]aurora ar**bor**+**real**+**is**]borealis.

The ordained ovate orifice oracle, **oral**+make+**did**]orated orthodox
oath, over oak.
Arms and h**A**nds **A**t **A**pex **A**bove at **A**ten RA's areola
aura+**Ra**]aurora, an **A**t+**land**+**is**)Atlantis in arctic air.

A+(**spr**ing+air)**spear**+**grass**]asparagus **spr**ing+**out**]sprouts like
aroused aimed Eros **air**+(**bent**+**low**)**bow**ed]arrows arcing like
arches in **arch**+**airy**]archery, and **flow**+**sky**+**wing**]flying like a
spear+**arrow**]sparrow.

Ancient celestial Incest **ancest**or+**Ra**+**elevate**]ancestral
down+**sent**+**acts**]decendents are **descend**ed+**ceased**]deceased.

Above art re**peat**+**arrangers**]rearrangers,
de+**arrangers**]dearrangers, **chi**+**arrangers**]changers architects.
Is **Is**+**Ra**+(**elevated**+**light**)**el**]Israels
arc-of-(**coven**+**act**]covenant/arch-of-covenant, an archaic
artifact? Is **kno**w+**all**]Noahs ark like a **new**+**over**+**above**]nova's
arc? Are
above+**round**+**change**)**arc**+**change**)**arch**+(**angle**+**elevate**)**angel**]a
rchangels, the **evening**+**angels**+**all**]evangelical
real+**elated**]related elevated+**legit**+**able**)eligible
elevate+**home**]Elohiem named Michael, Gabriel, Ishmael,
Ezekiel, Raphael, Daniel, and Emmanuel? El means "the" as in
Theos/God. Is it the **aged**+**elders**]angels,

change+**angels**]changels, who electrify **spit**+**arcs**]sparks across the sky?
Observe, the are the eldest elders of order of olden **old**+**in**]Odin/Woden are the **ele**vate+**ment**al+**are**+**thee**]elementary **element**+**angels**]elementals.

The Surname **Orion**+(**Sire**+**us**]Sirius/serious)**O**siris+**did**]sired us with desire to survive. Its sight is **sign**+**all**)**sig**nal+**high**]sigh insignia signature, **design**+**make**]designated, and significant. Olympus **o**round+**us**]Ouranus, over us, Above us, offers all organized order.

Overarching Above lights are arch angles, ancient ancestors Anastasi, Anunnaki and **high**+**arch**+**see**]hierarchy of Archon **all**+**thee**+**arch**+**see**]oligarchy and **air**+**one**]Aryan archetypes. **Fair**+**airy**]fairy are fair, they are nary nefarious.
Allow **art**+**cir**culation]articulation of artistic, autistic, authentic **author**+**write**+**be**]authority arrangers of artful **art**+**official**]artificial. **Astro**+**logo**s)**astro**logy+**name**+**see**]astronomy archaic arcane arching arcana, and **in**+**tell**)**intel**+**conn**ect+**you**+**all**]intellectual telling **intel**+**allegence**]intelligence was **cons**cious+**star**+**tell**+**make**+**shown**]constellations smart startling start to **arch**aic+**theology**]archeology, archeo-astronomy, and **astro**nomical+**theology**]astrotheology.
Then **chart**+**graph**ic+**see**]cartography, was carved of cartoon cartouche hieroglyph petroglyph art and artifacts are found of ancient, Argonaut, astronauts, **A**vatar+**alien**)**avi**an+**navig**ate)**aviate**+**repeat**]aviators and (**navy**+**aviate**)navig**ate**+**repeat**]navigators.

Reach the **Apex**+**attitude**]aptitude **up**+(**Alter**+**make**)alternate]ultimate ulterior All Allah good **God**+**old**]Golden, that alters **alternate**+**latitude**]altitude attitude. **At**+**tune**]attune and **at**+**lone**]Atone to **at**+**on**]Aton and become one with **At**+**Aten**)**attend**+**shown**)**att**ention+**aptitude**]attitude. See that attractive **at**+**man**)**Atm**an+**of**+**sphere**]atmosphere and **Atom**+**make**]Atomic is adamantly Adam, Ankh amulets for Atum, Amun Ra, **Amen**+**mend**]amend Om hum. So don't wait in **stop**+**at**]state with weight of hate, for all have slated late date with fate.

The Sanskrit, shelter called shala is now **shut+her]**shuttered but our shawl sheet shell still shields on our **shelf+holder]**shoulders. Shaman Sun of Egypt sees Hail high **At+up+Helios+on]**Aphelion apex, of heaven **A**bove.

Hoo**rah** all see eye of **Horus+rise+on]**horizon. Righteous Ra's reactor w**RA**th reigns, rages, and roars afar radiant rays that raise the rain of the **Ra+in+bow]**rainbow.

Auro**Ra** aura of Rama, and **Ra+Jah)Raja**s+land]Rajasthan rolling, ruling Shamesh, **S**hamash+one]sun, shining far asterisk southern star!

Shahs sultans shaman shastra shakymuni Shaolin priest and Shabbat salute Shangri La **Sha**mbala+om]Shalom Salaam peace. Shamus/sun/Shamash/Shemesh/ is **sun+shine]**sunshine/ **son+shrine]**sunshrine.

Sol+0m+on]Solomon/**soul+of+man]**Solomon of Shangri-La Shambala knows, Gnomon **shade+show]**shadow **sh**ow+man]shaman **sh**ows+good]should/**shove+good]**should/ **sh**ame+good]should **sh**ine+how)**sh**ow+all)**sh**all+care]share can+good]could will+good]would. But shazam! scandal is **sh**ame+scam]sham, **sh**ade+name]shame, **sh**un+aimed]shamed. It's a **b**lemish+name)**b**lame+under]blunder, a **b**lack+name]blamed as game like **b**low+fast)blast+fame+see]blasphemy that disclaims, maims defames, **fam**ily+you+are)**fam**iliar+of+us)**fam**ous+name]fame.

Shamans were **sh**adow+rounded]shrouded as **sh**ady+low+be]shadowy **sch**edule+theme]scheme screw scandal shenanigans shills of (**sh**aky+fl**abby**)**sh**abby+odd+be]shoddy made up **mask**ed+parade]masquerade, **st**op+dance]stance pretty+dance]prance that **par**ticipate+raid]parade and **ch**ant+neer]cheer the **ch**air+man]chairman's **ch**arlatan+(**party+raid**)parade]charade of fairly **c**aring+share+at+thee]charity.

Bible related words

Benevolent beliefs
benefitting+of**ficial**)**bene**ficial+**diction**]benediction of the
bi+**look**]book Bible of Babylon bitterly literally rhymes with lie libel.
Manipulated man bowed bended to and **be**+**lea**ded]believed
binding beliefs of the Bible's benevolent addiction,
false+**d**ic**tion**]fiction of predictions, longing to belong to beyond.
The grabbing+ga**sping**]grasping gothic golem
ga**ssy**+**gus**t+be]ghastly lost **gh**ost+**soul**]ghouls
growl+**moan**]groan discuss **dis**appointed+**gust**]disgust and
percussively cuss as they gather in gross gaping gaps to find and
fill exact cracks in the facts. They go gossip about the goals of the
holes in the (**God**+**host**)**gho**st+(**speak**+**tell**)**spells**]gospels, and
s**p**ot+**poof**]s**p**oof the s**p**irit+**kooky**]spooky spirit telling.

Appalling **appear**+**at**]apparent abhorrent aberrations of perished
apart particles **app**ear+**it**+s**hown**]apparitions with piercing peers
disperse, disappear, **e**nergy+**vapor**+m**ake**]evaporate and
energy+**vacu**um+m**ake**]evacuate.

Coverment Government

Listen to the great guttural disgruntled **growl**+**want**]grunt
growl+**rough**]gruff tough predator **prey**+**owl**]prowlers
hoot+**growl**]howl. It's the
grow+**moaning**]groaning+**howl**)**growl**+**dump**]grump of grampy
frumpy that **jolt**+**up**]jumps at **st**and+**up**]stumps stunts. But it's a
thump+**dud**/**dead**]thud of
trampled tricky **tr**avel+**up**]trump up trumpet trumpery.

Understand under the unending
universe+**all**)**universal**+**city**]university are
unite+**are**+**i**+**am**]Unitarian zen **city**+**sons**]citizens dwelling in
city+**dell**]citadel.
You are Yo**U**/**unique**+**one**]union with
Yo**uniqu**/)**unique**+**verse**]Universe/one song.
Well+**come**]welcome in to the inn, **be**+**unity**+**ful**]beautiful
come+**mu**tal+**unity**]community.

In common+(unit+tie)unity)community+make]communicate comment+demand]command comrade+are+we]comradery. See+ Essence+it+all)essential+is)essences)senses+all]sensual inner+cents+i+have]incentive of sent+intimate]sentiment sent+utterance]sentences. Will you resent that they repeat+present]represent 100 percent extra+central+magic]eccentric exist+essential]existential sense? Taste+essence]test and gut+(essence+make)estimate]guess query+essence]quest answers to the quest+shown]question.

C symbol is seen similar to a G Good, old, cold, gold cruely rules and rolls fools by old God of
Go+over+mind]government/ go+cover+mint]goverment is like covering+mind]covernment of coven+mind]covenment.
Its the over arch of the
curve+over)cover+inverted)covert+hidden)coven+act]covenant that cover+get]covet, cave+vortex]cavort, in ally+(cave+groove)cove]alcoves, groove+cove]grove and cave+in)cavern+land+yonder]canyons. It's a
curve+swirling]curling that connects chakras/circumfrence+curling]circling, whip+curling]whirling, twist+curling]twirling, swish+curling]swirling high+curling]hurling and spirit+all+swirling]spiraling.
It's a conscious+seal]conceals, conscious+affirms]confirms conscious+occur]concur con's conscious+travel+roll]control tool. Diplomats with diploma+see]diplomacy are dignified dignitaries with proven papyrus papers, paid by paying patriot pay+at+treat+on]patreons.

Connect+gregarious+essence]congress consciously regresses and connect+gregarious+make+did]congregated at conscious+spiral]conspire convene+shown]conventions. See senior senators have seen but are now sense+nil]senile putting oppressive news press+sure]pressure and conning congress and constantly, cause deep+pressing]depressing, super+pressing]suppressing and ante+agonizing]antagonizing aggressions.
Seek+cure)secure+of+thee]security provisions to providences provide+cure]procure proceed+(end+sure)endure]procedure for pure+fact]perfect cure.

The
pentagram+tentacle)pentacle+hogan)pentagon+house]penthou
se represents unrepentant repeating
serpentine+repetitious]surreptitious/
serpent+reptiles+is+shown]surreptitious
suspicious+inspect)suspect+end]suspend+sense]suspence to
repent sedicious in+side+of+us]insidious
suspect+i+see+of+us]suspicious is+spy+knowledge]espionage
of prying eyes of spot+eye)spy+hider]spiders and
sticks+snake]stake-out snake+seek]sneek
snake+vipers]snipers.
They project+rude)protrude and crud+rude]crude turning
prune+rude)prude into+rude+being]intruding low+crude]lewd.
Oodles of googols+ogling]googling, foggy goggled eyes catch of
prove+evoking]provoking poking meeting point, molten
smear+melting]smelting pot of inner+net]internet usurp,
survey+veil+acts]surveillance prevailing on we.

War Violence

Aristotle's aristocrats and Athens+elite]athletes compete to
advance to Alpha Acropolis of academy academics.
Admit+shown]admissions of
advance+minister+maker]administrators make
added+mirror+make+shown]admiration of
miracle+nebulous]miraculous Adonis
admirals mired in mere mirror+images]mirages of
miser+able]miserable misery.
The adore+minted/mental]adornments are
décor+made+did]decorated with fired+ore]forged
ore+of+mint]ornaments. The stagnant+hell]stale hole ore is a
metaphor, for molton
smoke+other]smother/smash+other]smother
smoke+(metal+welded)melded/melted]smelted
smoke+inhale]smell of war. Antagonist Hindu God of
fire/Agni+makes]agitates, Agni+grave+make]aggravates ignites
fire of antagonizing agony of protagonists.

The **feral+raucous**]ferocious, **fur+see)fury+in+us**]furious, force+right)**fight+stay**]feisty and fire+pi**erce**]fierce who **foes+fight**]fought make+r**ight**]might/**my+right**]might be down+**feeted**]defeated.

When fear enters it **enter+fears**]Interferes as a+**fear+raid**)afraid+(now+**ear**)near)fear+n**ight**]fright! If often offended, fen**ce+intend**]fend-off with **off+fence**]offenses and have **dee**p+**fence+end)defen**d+**l+have**]defensive trend for a bound+array]boundary.
See the illustrating illumination of instilled illusions. Evil **ill+legal**]illegal, **ill+leg**al+**it+make**]illegitimate, **ill+no+ess**ence]illness, of pillaging, illogical illicit **change+ill**]chill of rehabilitating debilitating deluded, deliberate liability of disabilities of insensibilities of **milit**ant+artill**ery**]military Kali/ **cut+ill**]killings. **I+no+fidelity**]infidelity **fall+ill/find+real**]feelings. They promising pricey **priv**ate+**leg**ura]privilege **syrup+prize**)surprise/**surge+prize**]surprise for first class privates irritable irritated raiding **pire+takes**]pirates who deal and steal.

Office+**all**)official +**doer**]officers often offer incentive and insensitively off men that offend or send men to end. Several sergeants in reserve severely sever and then are sent to serve segmented segregated secured section sector seats as senior senators.

Corporal **puni**tive+**sh**own+**ment**al]punishment for the incorporated co-opted **combined+operations**]cooperations of core of nations cohorts in cohoots with **core+operate+sh**own]corporations that collect **core+rupt**ure]corrupt profits from coroner reports of Marine Corps corpses in coffins. Misleading **miss**ion+project**iles**]missiles missed the missionary's mission.

Circle+**Ap**/up]**cap**+it+all)**Capital**)+i+am]capitalism is decapitated
If the head+(**cap**+it]hat gold **king**+dome]kingdom is not a good
God+olden]golden **wise**+dome]wisdom.

Active actors **at**+(**c**lose+aim)**claim**]acclaim with activating
act+shown]actions of **act**+(**show**+**all**)shall)**actual**+**see**]accuracy,
the **fact**+(**show**+**all**)shall]factual
actual+(**real**+**it**+be)real**ity**]actuality.

Month "ides of March", named for **mar**vel+of+**us**]marvelous God
of war **Mars**+ring]marring, **Mars**+crun**ching**]marching maiming
afar. **Gory**+ki**ller**]gorilla's and **armor**ed+be]armies armed with fire
arms armaments are disarmed and **down**+**feet**+**did**]defeated. .
The hit **hard**+**shown**+**see**]harshly **host**ile+eng**age**]hostages
hold+m**eld**)**held**+jail]hell.

Jehovah, Jesus Jupiter, judge+ment]judgments of
juries+dictate+shown]jurisdictions justly adjudicate judicial
judged+**stop**+ce**ace**]justice without **pre**vious+**jud**ge+**us**)**prej**udice
for **per**petrator+**jury**]perjury, and judiciously **just**+**i**+**find**]justify that
suspects adjust to **just**ice+**cell**]jail sealed in hell. They conduct a
reconnaissance and reconsider and reconcile
consider+make)**con**ciderate+**census**]consensus to for
sentencing.

Some devolved deplorable **du**plex+soli**citous**]duplicitous
mischief+**evil**+**is**]mischievous
down+(**ev**ening+**ill**)**evil**)**devil**+**is**]devious
demon+**mon**ey+seek]demonic **vile**+**man**]villians defile the village.

Devious+vile)de**vil**+**men**]villains are
inner+**vol**untarily+**did**]involved in violet
violent+**take**)**viola**te+**reptile**]volatile acts of
violent+silence]violence. They become
Suspect+**vicious**]suspicious convicts without
conscious+**vin**dications]convictions who

in+timid+make]intimidated **vict**ory+**tim**id]victims. They are mostly lazy **mal**aise+**functioning**]malfunctioning **male**+**violent**]malevolent males, dismal **maul**+vi**cious**]malicious incriminated **creep**+**took**]crooks and **crim**e+(**ani**mated+**maul**)**animals**]criminals have grinning grimey **grim**+**face**]grimaces full of animus and malice with no discrimination. They find the **feel**+**line**]feline, **feel**ing+**male**]females/ **feed**+**male**]female **feed**+**men**+**in**]feminine with mammary mammal breasts.

They will **scar**+**rape**]scrape and **scald**+(talk+old)**told**]scold with **scar**+**tab**)scab+scarlet)**scar**+**very**]scary, **scar**+**torn**]scorn.

Don't grimly gripe or **grief**+**I**+**have**]grieve, but receive, perceive and **be**+**lie**+**have**]believe with no conceited exception, your **prev**ious+**conceive**]preconceived perception of achieving, is a demon deceived deception by usurping circling serpents **serp**entine+(repeating+it+is)**repetitious**]surreptitious reptiles. Instead **receive**+**scepter**]receptor to receive **red**eemed+conte**mpt**+**shown**]redemption. **Conception**+**dam**]condoms **con**vict+**damn**]condemn intercept **concept**+**shown**]conception of **inner**+**section**]intersection/ **inner**+**sex**]intersex **erect**+**shown**)erection+**rupt**ure+**shown**]eruption.

Brutish **brute**+**all**)**brutal**+**right**]bright Brutus bothering **brother**+**rat**]brats ab**normal**+**use**]abuse and **brutal**+**use**)bru**ise/** They **bat**+**her**]batter and **beat**+(whip+belt]welt. Their **whip**+**on**]weapons and **bomb**astic+**hard**]bombarding burning and burying is an **a**+**bombin**g+**made**+**shown**]abomination.

Spiked spears of spastic **spar**ing+**man**]Spartans like stems, stalks, straws, sticks, stakes and stab in **jab**+**in**]javelins jab+gouge+st**aff**]joust stay off the **stav**e+**off**)staff+**jabs**)stabs+**jag**]stag.

Romantic **Rome**+**man**]Roman ruler Romulus rained down and reigned and ruled with rules sees **seiz**e+**Czar**]Caesar seizures easily increased. Later they named August for Augustus and July for Julius. But they did not justice to nature question for they did not understand equinox procession.

Vigorous **vict**or+g**lorious**]victorious **V**ict**ory**+**kings**]Vikings of **val**ley+**hall**+**all**]Valhalla evict and **inn**er+**timid**+**made**]intimidated and convicted victims.
View vengeful revenge vendetta and revere valiant vigilante's **vigil**+(s**ealed**+**lips**)si**lence**]vigilance.

Like a **scr**am+h**urrying**]scurrying harried hare, the **horror**+**finding**]horrifying **horror**+**did**]horrid **horror**+**able**]horrible hairy horde came like a **hurry**+**came**]hurricane/ **horror**+**came**]hurricane. Like a hurling **hurt**+**arm**]harming, **hide**+thee+**us**]hideous, huge+**bulk**)hulk, **hung**+m**onkies**]hunks hid+**cuddled**]huddled. Hundreds of huge+**bulk**]hulk musty+h**usky**]musky men **sink**+**duck**]sunk un**der** beneath+(**hide**+b**unch**)h**unch**+**under**)h**unker**]bunker, h**un**kering+**wanting**)h**unting**+**angry**]hungry hitting and hurting.

The **tight**+m**an**)t**itan**+gig**antic**]titanic makes **tiger**+**raid**]tirades and takes and tears terrestrial territory and t**ake**+**axe**}taxes and tariffs. The t**iara**+**rant**]tyra**nt** is a **tear**+**repeat**)t**error**+**able**]terrible ty**ranny**+m**onsoon**]tyfoon that causes **tear**+**roar**]terrorists, terrorizing with tear+**l**+**finding**)t**errifying**+**roar**+**l**+**am**]terrorism.

The **net**+**work**]network of **war**d+**den**]warden **war**+**lock**]warlock/ **war**+**locked**]worked for warship, warhead awards and waged war afar. But see **sore**+**woe**]sorrow and **woe**+**sorry**]worry of **worn**+**leery**]weary **war**+**recur**]warriors who's army **war**+(**hurt**+**arms**)**harms**]warns of the wordsmith's **word**+**ship**]worship at **work**+(**show**+**open**)**shops**]workshops.

Paternal Politics

Grace+s**how**+**us**]gracious **great**+**garish**]gregarious grandiose gray gay guy Gregory, is **pop**+**pole**+**are**]popular pastor, pontificating Pontiff, Papa Pope. So, Pope Gregory reformed gold mine tool time now golden church holidays control the mind.

Zeus is **Jump+up+pater**]Jupiter is Father paternity. **Pater+all)pat**ernal+**riot)pat**riot+**arch)pat**riarch+(**cont**inue+**rule**)c ont**rols**]patrols the publishing of the popular public people in the **populat**e+**shown**]population in pubs and pubelos.

Partisan party counterpart **partners+ship**]partnerships participate and **part+take**]partake and intake in taking apart parting article art.They are the paying who **pay+true+ones)patrons+eyes**]patronize pay tolls of the **oppos**ed+**sit**]opposite **pole**+opposite+**all**]political **pow+re**peat]power polite politicians. The ones who manage **mono+pole+energy**]monopoly money of **met**ered+cont**rol)metro+police**]metropolis and its please **pole+light)polit**e+**nice**]police. It's the **pole+peace+says**]policies that push with puny impunity and immunity and they punitively disrupt. They abruptly erupt and corruptly **punch+r**upture]puncture with **pun**ish+crun**ch)punch+i+shown)punish+minds**]punishments. They **push+at**]put prisoners in **sus**tained+**pen+shown**]suspension in **pens+is**]penis+**all)pen**al+**tent+are**a]penitentiary.

Come+ap**prehend**]comprehend **parent+thesis**]parenthesis and **common+pair**]compare **pair+like+rail**]parallel parts. They punish **perver**se+**turn**]pervert pedophile **treachery+r**eason]treason traitors and prosecuting purposeful perpetrators but parse **pared+down**]pardons for padded prodigal **pat**riot+**ones**]patrons.

Muddy money spins spine spindle of Up/**Ap**+fall**ing**]Appalling political polished pole dance politicians of balanced ballot poll. **Pre+steed+stag+is**]prestigious pumped pompus precedent **previous+sid**ing+**sent**]president POTUS **cand**or+**did)cand**id+**mates**]candidates doing caped capers and

escape+made]escapades for electric **elector+all**]electoral
seal+**election**]selection.

The tasks mask lie in the sun basking of passing the basket.
The suspicious+pros**pect**]suspects commence commerse
serpent representation. They defend pensive apprehensive
pending penned misspending on **deter+fence**]defense pen and
extended lending or suspend **ex**tra+**spend+i+have**]expensive
stipend that ends in uptrend in that send plenty pleasant presents.
They pen in **in**ner+**depend+dance**]independence,
come+pen+satiate]compensates companions with pending
pensions. Some aim to suspend end compensation SS pensions
and cents of peasants? Hence, does
pen+all)penal+tent+i+porary]penitentiary penance make sense
or dense nonsense? Repent with **pre**side+**sense**]presence and
common+ap**prehend**]comprehend. **Pay+in**]pain of panacea
pandoras box **pai**n+m**anic)pan**ic+en**demic**]pandemic
panorama+**demon+i+am**]pandemonium is **fr**ight+**end+see**]frenzy
of **fear+night)fr**ight+(**pai**n+m**anic)p**anic]frantic.
Polemic+lun**atic+all**]political politicians make
pole+eyes+make+**shown**]polarization, but bipolar **no+pole**]nope
and **yes+p**ole]yep is one pole spinning in the same direction.
Interpret+**pole+make**]interpolate fate. If the **top+pole**]topples it
tips the **tim**e+**pole**]temple of the **steep+pol**e]steeple and
church+**pole**]chapel and **pole+pits**]pulpits in the metropolis.
All lulled by call of tall wall that won't fall.
A disposed **come+posed**]composed imposter with
in+posing]imposing poised posture proposes purposes
not+probe+able]improbable. They are improvable
not+purpose+**able)imp**ossible+**caus**e]implausible, impassable in
opposed+**site**]opposite **pose+sit+shown**]position.

Ayn+Rand]Aryan Barbarian Bavarian hard line harbor embargo,
they **fashion+brick+make**]fabricate block rocks that bar lock
block.a **bar**bed+stoc**kade**]barricade. It's a hard barring barrage of
fugitive refugees from barrio barrens barging over the boarder, to

get beyond the barrier bars in a **bar**ter+**gain**]bargain bet to be better. It's an arduous banter for banning and banishing bands of famished **dam**ned+**aged**]damaged, **band**ana+**aided**]bandaged band aid **un**der+**bash**ful]unabashed banshees and **bad**+hab**its**]bandits and **band**ana+idi**ots**]bandits.

Society's Drugs Horrors Crimes

So+**high**]sigh about **inner**+**hailing**]inhaling **in**+**scents**]incense of **high**+**per**son]hyper E**gypt**+**see**]gyps**ies**.
They held**+old**]hold+**ope**n)**hope**+**full**]hopeful tie-dyed **happy**+tr**ippy**)h**ipp**ie+(**knot**/**know**+**l**)**eyes**+**did**]hypnotized by **hyper**+**know**+**is**)**gnosis**]hypnosis. They were hazed dazed crazed at the hopping happening. They see saw **psyche**+**delic**acies]psychedelic of **cyclic**+**of**+**log**ic]cyclology/ **psych**olog**y**+log**ical**]psychological **hyp**ed+(**critical**+**eyes**)criticize+**crazy**]hypocrisy.

No, nada, naughty, **not**+**either**]neither **not**+**ever**]never **not**+**tasty**]nasty, narcissistic, **nause**ous+**making**]nauseating, not cool Jule/jewel, fools fools. **Drag**+**on**]dragon of **sig**nal+**erect**)**cig**arette+(**tacky**+**char**)**tar**]cigar **chal**k+**tar**]**char**+**coal**]charcoal nicotine, fiend to **cough**ing+**in**]coffin. Needless narcoleptic narcotics, with obscene **need**+**hole**]needles see end of friend **end**+**of**+**me**]enemy energy. They develop into homeless hopeless slippery slope of enveloping dope.

Like pots of pot **potent**+event**ually**]potentially **potent**+**shown**]potions, emit **emo**+**evoke**)**emo**te+**shown**]emotion/ **energy**+(**moon**+**ocean**)**motion**]emotion. It motivates **mini**+**minute**]minutes moments movements with momentum and moves like movies and mobile motors.
Divine+**out**)**dev**out+**em**ot**ion**]devotion devoured **devout**+**be**]devotees devoted to find inner **de**termined+**fine**]defined **divine**+**made**+**shown**]divination.

My **Moon+day]**Monday mode **brown+(mind+moved)mood]**broods
and moves with loony lunatic Lunar Luna/Sin -name of Babylon
moon) and stirs the **moon+theos+see]**monthly
moon+stir]monster.

My **neighbor+hood]**neighborhood **Robbinh+in+hood]**Robinhood
hooligan **hood+bum]**hoodlum is hidden in hideouts wearing
hoodies, holding hideously high, hoodoo voodoo goodies.

Hole+wore)whores**+moan]**hormonal ho's sell self to bored
abhorrent groaning horny hordes.
Some **slide+cut]**slut whores are **horror+make+all+be]**horrifically
held hostage by the horrible hostile brothers, bought by buying
bronco **broth**er**+hotel]**brothel. They originate oral orifice
organisms and **A.I.D.S** and often offer officer's orgiastic organ
orgasms at raids.
Pervasive adverts subvert persuade with powerful purveyors' porn
covertly converts perpetrators, the love forlorn.
Eros+rouse]arouse raises excites **erect+make]**erotic exotic
creates exoteric esoteric **ecst**atic**+fant**asy**]**ecstasy.
Controversially overtly coming over like a complex sexual hex, a
vexing vertical fluctuating vertex vortex vertigo cumming reflex.
Diverting reverting extraverts into inverted, introverted perverts!

Straggley, Raggedy Ann Rock & **str**ut**+roll]**strolls, with
sway**+bag]**swag they irrationally erratically
sway**+stagger]**swagger, stumbling **tri**cking**+fli**pping**]**tripping
strung out unzipper. Act as **str**ipper**+p**uppet**]**strumpets for Jack-
off the raping ripper jipping tippers. They rip off strip straps, to
strobe light flashes. See G string strands, sexy glances, they
strut**+gli**ding**]**striding, striking stances. They trap sad saps in lap
trap dances making stubble studs grow sturdy strong.
Some are **sin+l+stir/st**ore**]**sinister **sin+phallus]**syphilis sinners.
Others chug-a-lugged drink **jar+m**ugs**]**jugs of ta**boo+ooze]**booze
become **cause+sick)**caustic nox/**n**auseous**+toxic+us]**noxious
in+(toxin**+sick)toxic+ate+did]**intoxicated **drow**n**+hazy]**drowsy

(drain+down)drown+hug)drug+funk]drunk. Some pop powerful powder pay+in]pain bad+ill]bills for pills of push+open)pop)+seeds]poppies and yucky fucking sucking jumpy+flunkies]junkie monkeys shoot mugging thug drugs. They risk chain reigns, tied tangent+angles]tangled knee+angle]kneeling with down+hanging]dangling wrangled in deranged+anger]dangers of agrivated+pressure+have]aggressive strain+juggle]struggle choking wrong strong+mangle]strangle/strap+angle]strangle strange strain+anger]strangers.

Drop draw+cape]drapes drawn at dawn. The dream+dead]dread of lay+anguish]languishing in being anxious+I+see]anxiety+grieve+injury]angry of down+anger]dangers from strain+anger]strangers is a dramatic+spastic]drastic tragic+drama]trauma of karma.

Prostrating+institute]prostitutes and people of problems, prodigal procreated+generation+thee]progeny have few prospects to prosper in poor+invert+thee]poverty. They can end up persecuted+sued]pursued probable+((electric+(axe+cut]executed)electrocuted]prosecuted, with jump+volt]jolts.

Some seek to asset+social+make]associate asset+similar+make]assimilate in asinine same asylum. Others assaulters assumed at fault are assembled into insane asylums.

Some are double+be+is]dubious, demoralizing demagogue+god]demigod mob+monster]mobster and bang gang+monster]gangsters and demonetizing ranking bank+trickster]banksters, barricading in build+under]bunkers.

They run a foul and are flunky flat+fails]flailing fell+one]felons with a fell+lonely]felony.

Despite causing despair, disrepair and demise, like despised, despicable, desperate desperado's, dispirited despots, they are like **dragon+i+am**]draconian Dracula in medieval dungeon. They dramatically, drastically, drag, draw, **down+rain**]drain, drink the drilled **spill+oil**ed]spoils of the demolished, tormented turmoil and tilling+soil]toil of disposed **destr**uct+**noise**+did]destroyed soil.

They do Illegal divisive designs that divulge, divert, devastate, devour, defile, devoid the divine.

I **add+damn+see**]adamantly add, that **dem**ons+com**anding**]demanding+**monst**er+m**aking**]demonstrating men with mean **down+meaning**]demeaning demeanor leanings diverge to di**vide+force**]divorce **De**mon+**crazy**]democracy. They de**termines+sides**]decides di**vide+vision**]division with libations deliberately liberate to **divid**e+**ends**]dividends.

They **dim+min**imize+**sh**ow]diminish demented **dumb+ment**al+**l**+have]dementia deceptions and **different+ment**al+**shown**]dimensions, of nonsymmetrical diameters from **divi**ded+**angle**)**dia**gonal+ca**bol+it+all**]diabolical di**vide+ab**ove+**below**]diablo's diametric double dealings. They **defy+not**]definatly and defiantly determine derived and**d**evolved+**illusion**]delusion **defin**e+it+**shown**]definition conclusion.

Environmental Degradation

We can grapple, **great+need**)**greed+have**)**gra**b+cla**sp**]grasp, **sm**all+w**ack**)**sm**ack+**fight**]smite **st**ep+**romp**]stomp, **sm**all+**push**)**sm**ush+**trash**]smash bash, back stab brush aside, and bushwhack it. We can chain, **stretch+pain**]strain, **spr**ing+**pain**]sprain, or **squ**eeze+**smash**]squish it. But if we fucking fricking **fra**cture+**crack**]frack nature in cranny cr**ease+abyss**]crevices. It **cr**acks+**bunchs**]crunchs breaks and **crack+**(roll+**tumble**]rumbles]crumbles into rubble of creation. It creates batches of hash **tramp+ash**]trashed **smash+push**]smush **cr**ash+**rush**)**cr**ush+**wrinkle**]crinkled with kinks, **crack+dust**]crust,

a **cr**ud+**rude**]crude grime nation. It makes earthquake
shake+qu**iver**]shiver shudder **sh**ake+**rift**)**sh**ift+**after**]shaft
drag+**rift**]drift and forward+ba**ll**)fa**ll**+**tumble**]fumble.

So raise **ram**ification+**parts**]ramparts and
parameter+**rim**]perimeter brim making a **b**ind+**ridge**]bridge,
bench, beach.
Become rambunctious, **ram**+**rage**]rampage
roar+**wave**)rave+**ch**ant]rant **raven**+**us**)**ravenous**+sav**age**]ravage
because **rave**+eng**age**)**rage**+**ape**)**rape**+**is**]rapist ripping
rake+**keep**)**reap**+**taking**]raking.

So reasonable revolution raises rational running renegades under
radar rascal radicals **ra**diating+d**azzle**]razzle/**Ra**+**soul**]razzle radio
frequencies and rapping raspy rhapsodies that TMI, Chernobyl
fuck+**you**+**sh**ow+**ma**]Fukushima radioactive unclear
new+**clear**]nuclear reactor rainfall is rancid. The loud atom bomb
mushroom **sh**oulder+**cloud**]shroud muffin puff was like a macabre
macaroon monsoon muff. It's **dr**ip+pl**op**]drop of dismal
drop+**fizzles**]drizzles of rain is a nebulous nimble numbing nimbus
nemesis.
So **pro**tect+**test**]protesters playtesting taking
testy+state**ments**]testaments and tasty testimony.
Usher in useful united utopian uproar undermining mining
uranium.

Rather than **rat**ify+**sh**own+**eyes**]rationalize, real relatives really
real+**eyes**]realize the **law**+(**lie**+**repeater**)**lier**]lawyer's lie in
labyrinth lairs of libelous lies.
Legions of litigious, illegal illegitimate lawyers deregulate the
legara+**all**]legal laws of leagues of **leg**al+**it**+**make**]legitimate
legal+**state**+**doers**]legislators.
This allows, outlaw low lying awful **law**+**full**]lawful flawed laws that
a**ll**+(**lead**+**edge**)**ledge**]allege ledgers.

But **bull**+**i**+**close**]bellicose **re**vel+**bulls**]rebels
bull+**lig**ature+**relent**+**see**]belligerently bow to rulers' rules. Does

the raucous rally require **revo**lt+so**lution**]revolution? Right wing
white Reich elections enriches the right and leaves the labor left.
Re**pulsive**+(pig+**ug**ly)**pug**+**act**]repugnant
repress+**sent**+i+**have**]representitives
re**peating**+**public**+i+**am**]Republican in pubs publicly
public+i+**sh**ow]publishes rubbing **regime**+**mind**]regimented
required **regular**+**make**)**regulate**+**did**]regulated
regulate+**shown**]regulations are **rubb**le+pub**lish**]rubbish.

Rita's **cor**related+**right**)cor**rect**+**story**)**rector**+**be**]rectory rectifies
and **resume**+**erect**]resurrects, wrong **right**+**be**+**us**]righteous
writings that lift+**read**]lead, respect and revive
seek+**quest**)sequestered+(**write/rites**+**you**+**all**)**ritua**ls)se**cret**s of
re**gal**+**gala**)regalia+**lig**ature+**shown**]religion that revel in revered
reverend **re**+**veiling**]revealing revelation. They
proclaim+**loud**)proud+raise)**praise**+**say**)**pr**ay+**hear**)prayer+**reach**]
preach and talk+**each**]teach with a
pray+per**formance**]prayerformance.

The propagate segregated deregulated delegate readily relegate.

The ordained ruler's **aim**+**bit**+**sh**own]ambition is to rule and
rollover with rules and reign down like rain with
constrict+**rein**]constraining **ch**ange+**reins**]chains to
rest+**strain**]restrain and arrange range of the range.
They **repeat**+**tr**y+**brain**]retrain, **down**+**rain**]drain
repeat+(**ob**ligate+**gain**)ob**tain**]retain and ingrain stain your brain.
They **extra**+**plain**]explain the profane with insane/unsame inane,
game to **certi**fy+ob**tain**+**see**]certainly sustain your in inner pain.
They
entertain+n**ice**)entice+(**in**+cen**ter**)**enter**+**obtain**]entertain/inner
tame with **inner**+(**at**+**gain**)attain+**ment**al]entertainment that
contains tainted saint contamination to **close**+**aim**]claim your brain
and leave remnant remains.

Television Advertising Consumerism

Tell+a+vision]television inner+still]instills and keeps the tube turned, tuned to permanent+turbulent]perturbed turmoil dissed+turbulent]disturbed divided+vison]division.
We see simulated sin+theos+make]synthetic cynical TV, sinful insincere cinema.
See simple similar+tool)symbol+magic]symbolic symbiotic Simpsons show is simpleton subtle subdued sublime sub+limit+minimal]subliminal simulating similar symptoms of social+I+see]society.
When we keep tabs on tabloid on tablets tabs,
they profit from victims of conning convicted, they have no conscious or convictions. They tantalize with tantric tranquil in+chant+sing]enchanting trances and dances.

Attractive active acting actors avert us to enticing, exciting controversial eye lies diversion advertisements, that confine adapt adopt me+eye]my mind's eye with comments from common+panel]companies. The community+merchandise)commerce+show+all]commercials are fun epiphanies for consumers to hear the barker's bark that marks the mark+get]market with merchant+paradise]merchandise.
When we pursue purse+chase]purchase and put it in poke or pack+it]pocket our money is socked away in sack or locked in locket!

See the distressing dressed to impress+shown]impression heredity+empress]heiress of the implied impermanent emperor+pyramid]empire.

Fasten+see+did]fascinated fanning fannie fan+estatic]fanatics that follow hollow fans+see]fancy fun faint/phantom+see)fantasy+(pliable+mastic)plastic]fantastic flow+fast+shown)flash+shown]fashion trends.
Connect+influence]confluence as affected+flow+dance]affluence a form of up/Ap+flu+za/end]Afluenza. The abiding buying austere rich hide like ostracized, ostriches. The plush pleasing please+sure]pleasure/play+sure]pleasure ploy boys pals pay for play at playa palaces.

The **snake+peek**]sneaks and **crawl+sneak**]creeps. We can
snag+(**cat+chase**)catch)**snatch**))+**drag**]snag, or
scrape+**catch**]scratch, snare, or **trick+snap**]trap it. We can
catch+**got**)caught or **snip+clap**)snap+latch)catche]snatch, as a
snack+pack)snack.
The **snub**+(**know+able**)noble)**snob**+**bark+be**]snarky
snub+(**object+i+have**)objective)**snob+hide**)snide+**jeers**)sneers+f
licker]snickers, **snout+roar**)snoar+short]snorts sniff+**huffs**]snuff
then (**snooty+out**)snout+got)snot+b**reezes**]sneezes.
Extra+(**spill+end**)spend+**I+have**]expensive sends away
my+need]money. So insure no **be+tra**der+all]betrayal and assure
ample trade **true+sure**]treasure.

Find the **pyramid+fire**]pyre of the empyrean empire and
stick+**poke**]stoke **fuel+spire**]fire of pyrotechnic desire inside
flow+glittering]flittering **flexing+lux**]fluxing
fire+lick+repeat]flickering/**flame+wicking**]flickering by
repeat+**flakes+spec+ing**]reflecting.

The inner **Ide+enter+thee**]identity in
id+is+ot]idiot/**idea+ot**]idiot is nothing, it's zero/0/ot/null thought
ideas. So they idolize **pop+you+are**]popular
id+doll/**eye+**doll)**idol+a+tre**asure]idolatry of
mod+(**idea+real**)ideal]model/ **mod+**doll]models, indulged idle
dolls.

Diss+cuss+being]disgusting customs of continuously consuming
upper crust customers, to **not+ever**]never feel fed fueled
fully+**filled**]fulfilled in their large volume **vac**ant+**rooms**]vacuums.
So they fill **vacant+sees**]vacancies on vicarious voyeuristic tourist
voyage tour **vacat**e+**shown**]vacations.

Social society **increase+climes**]inclines then **re**cline+**laxs**]relaxs
then **down+climes**]declines.
They long for illustrious elusive bueno, **boon+us**]bonus luck for
luxury of Luxor, to (**lay+ea**sy)**lazy+fair**]Laissez-faire
lay+sure]leisure in lush lustful lavish lounge life.
Then covering **cower+hunch**]crouch on
cushy+**i+on**)cushion+**slouch**]couch.

Mangling **maniac+all**]maniacal
hu**man+in**festations]manifestations, with, masked mannequins
made up with makeup in manufactured manicured mansions
without emancipating mandalbrot **manu**al+**script**]manuscripts on
their telling mantels.

Communication and Joke words

Conscious+**fuse+us**]Confucius contributed a
profuse+shown]profusion of **con**trol+**close**+al**lusion**]conclusions
of **con**scious+**fuse**d+**shown**]confusion of
down+**illusion**s]delusions. He is the founder of
conscious+**founding**]confounding profane profound sound
foundation.

Penned opined **open**+i+own]opinions are optional
optimum+**mystic**)**optimistic**)+**all**]optimistical or
infected+**pest**+**shown**]infestation an infested
pestilence+**of**+**myst**ery+make]pessimistic.

Don't be muffled by **muzzle**+one]Muslin
masked+**par**ty+r**aid**)parade]masquerade.

The extra+ordinary]extraordinary
sign+experi**ence**]science/**see**+in+ess**ence**]science experts
extra+**speak**+**cite**+**see**]explicitly explore and
extra+**speak**+**plan**]explain. They **spe**ak+**cite**+**c**ircle]specific
special **spe**ak+**open**]spoken spitting **sp**ew+**it**)spit+st**utter**]sputter
spiteful **sp**eak+**teach**]speech.
They **reach**+(**see**+**ear**+ch**ange**)**search**]research
beg+**seek**+**search**]beseech, **speak**+**out**]spout, **shut**+**out**]shout of
my+**out**]mouth, **d**own+**spit**+**puke**]dispute, refute
down+in**side**+**repel**]dispel **d**own+**speak**+**able**]despicable
spit+**squirt**]spurts of spilled **ex**it+**repel**+**did**]expelled
speak+**tell**]spell and tells to **di**scuss+**tales**]details.

A **tweet+(glow+litter/letter)glitter)twit**ter+**ch**ange]twitch is like a witches wish.

Joy+spoke)joke+folly)jolly+poke)joke+(laugh+ears)leers]jeers **snide+jeers]**sneers let buffoon+**(fun+be)funny]**phony fool make a jovial **happy+joke]**hoax. The joker+**gestures]**jester's **prove+(point+joke)poke]**provoke **speak+evoke]**spoke **energy+voice+spoke]**evoke with inner+**joy]**enjoy, and **joy+in)join+to)joint+stop]**joist **repeat+joy+voice]**rejoice at the **jubil**ant+be]jubilee.

They **be+most]**boast **bright+flag]**brag, **blow+gab]**blab, then **back+toward+be]**backwardly, **back+sh**ame+**full]**bashfully become **I'm+bare+ass+did]**embarrassed.

Loud+gaff]laugh+(aft+repeat)after]laughter ha ha **high+laugh+variously]**hilariously lulled to **close+slap)clap+loud]**applaud. The **audio**+attend**ance]**audience/**aud**ible+**silence]**audience in the **audio**tory+a**trium]**auditorium **audio+shown]**audition was in audacious awe.

Good **rid+dance]**riddance to their reduced redundant **ridicule+us]**ridiculous riddles.

Journey Through the Seasons of the Year

Christ+i+am]Christians of **ch**urch+**pole]**chapel **pole+pit]**pulpit see **cry+stop]**Christ is son of **Christ+mas**s]Christmas of noel **nat**al+**activity]**nativity and **imma**nent+ej**aculate]**immaculate exception no ejaculate injection, no worm+squ**iggle]**wiggle squ**i**ggle+worm]squirm sp**i**ll+germ]sperm **con**scious+**see+i+have]**conceive **concept+shown]**conception.

Peer+see+i+have]perceive my **peer+concept+shown]**perception is **inner+scept**er+**shown]**inception. Don't disbelieve, **be+come]**become and **belief+i+have]**believe I revealed shown **de**ceive+con**cept+shown]**deception.

That the **extra+crucial+making**]excruciating **cross+X]crux crucify+fix**ture]crucifix to crypt to rise rebirth created a crippling cringe and **cry**ing+**isis**)crisis. But, **critic+I+am)crit**isim+**eyes**]criticize chronic not+credit+able]incredible credence to **cri**me+an**imal**]criminal **cruc**ify+par**ades**]crusades of **hypnotic+eyes)hypnotized+crit**ical]hypocrite/ **hyp**er+**of+crit**ic)hypocrite oligarchs, monarchs, Patriarchs against atheist antichrist anarchists. Those who down+pro**nounce**]denounce, renounce **pro**claim+**noun**]pronounce **a+noun+see+make**]annunciate acclaim, notably with **note+right+be**]notoriety, that **Chi+rise+stop**]Christ as Sun is pronounced c-r-i-s-t as in crystal. It is the **frozen+mist**]frost at **cryst**al+**mist**]cristmist/Christmas that **mark+X**]marks, the crucial **crux+stop+mast**]Xmas of clear crisp snowflake **win**d+**term**]winter **Sol+st**op]solstice. The time when **twi**ce+**st**op)**tw**ist+(**wh**eel+cur**ling**)wh**irling**]twirling winding **whirl+old**]world the Earth makes rolling **rose+crux+i+am**]Rosicrucian ring around the rosy sun center. It's the crystal light **coron**a+**net)coronet+round**]crown sun king whos apparent motion appears to fall down when the Earth criss-crosses the neXus like a hex sign of Chinese XI/Chi/qu. The **Chi+arrange]ch**ange+**racing**]chasing **ch**ange+**barge**]charging energy flow direction to down V Vinter/**win**d+**turn**]winter with **blow+qu**icks]blitz and **blow+dust**y]blustery **sn**ot+**blow**]snowing **blow+hazzard**]blizzards and loose a**va**ult+**launch**]avalanche lunges **d**own+**luge**]deluges. Our **holy+orders**]hours are repeat+i+see]rise of time **ch**ange+**turn**ing]churning Earth.

This syndicated syncretism synopsis synthesis, shows a **sync+chrono**logic+**make**]synchronistic **Sun+day's**]Sunday is **sanct**uary+**mono+I+is**]sanctimonious **sacred+crucified+see)sac**rifice+**red)sac**red+**ment**al]sacrament. Does the forsaken suffering suffice as a **save+your/save+i+are**]savior to **save+flavor**]savor as salvia salve for savage sin and win saved+aged)**salva**ge+**shown**]salvation? Is Son Jesus of soul and **Jew**+**rule**+**salam**/*peace*]Jerusalem **s**imilar+**n**ame)same **s**imilar+**n**ame+in]synonym for savior Savitri Jewel+Ra+ (Sol+Om+man]Solomon Sun?

Down **ev**ening+**il**]evil is a simple **sublime**+**all**]subliminal **sym**bol+**biotic**]symbiotic simulating similar, **Descent**+**round**)**Down**+**arc**)dark **d**own+**sun**]done, the Set/Sat of the sun.
Synonymous Egyptian God Set of the dark underworld looks like a Satyr dressed as a red devil **s**ane+qu**aint**)**Sa**int+**en**d]Satan.
Sat is synonymous with end of week **Sat**+**urn**)**Saturn**s+**day**]Saturday, named after God Saturn/Father Time/**Chronos**+the**ology**]chronology. He cronically chronicals and syncronizes cronologial time. Saturn is also related to, the end of year festival of saturnalia, **sabbat**h+**l**+**cal**l]sabbatical, **sabot**a+**age**]sabotage, and symbolic of grim reaper of death with **s**ickle+**cy**cle+kn**ife**]scythe.
Coincidently the same red, satin suit clothes are worn at the end of the year by good kid cause **s**aint+**A**bove)**S**anta+**c**lose+**p**ause]Clause. He is the sane sanitary saint Nicolas of frosty **Cryst**al+**mas**s]Christmas. He is jangling Chris **chr**istmas+(**jolly**+(**tin**ge+tick**le**)**ti**ng**le**)jingle]Cringle/ **cri**nge+wr**inkle**)**cri**nkle+**tingle**]Cringle with **tw**ice+(**w**ince+bl**ink**)**w**ink+**able**]twinkle **g**iving+**lifts**]gifts.
He is of **No**+**re**peat+**theta**]north node N the land of know naught, 0, no sun, where Nederland/Netherlands/neverland, where Normandy Norms, Norway Norwegians, and Nordic are from.

Pig+**nor**th+**act**]ignorant **pagan**+**l**)pagani **N**+**all**/**Oll**)**n**o+**theos**)**N**orth+(**O**+**N**)**on**+**energy**)**one**]none, IN hid nil. **N**orth recognizes **cog**nitive+**relate**]cognate **cau**se+**notations**]connotations **con**scious+**knit**/**net**/**t**ie)connect+**shown**]connection **core**+**right**)**correct**+**relates**]correlates **n**+**ought**]not knot knit net **inner**+**net**]internet.

To fro+come]from beforeTwo-faced God
a+know+logic)analogy+eyes]analyze
Janus's+annual+reverse)anniversary]January resets times
Chronos+logical]chronological chrome
in+(come+pass)compass]encompasses and
circular+makes]circulates the
circle+come+reference]circumference of the circle+us]circuses
of circle+common+stance]circumstances. It's a 12 inner
circle+enter)center+all]central circumfrence+arc+all]circle.
These passion words of post pass+stop]past age page that
have+old]holds passwords to path+way/pass+age]passage. The
I inside Abracadabra+axis]Abraxas 3D complete+hex]complex.

See E early East entry, even event engine
Horus+is+risen]horizon sunrise for tells of
over+above+torus]oraborus.
Horus+(tell+scope)telescope]horoscope zoo+ark]zodiac of
haven+even]heavens of whole+sum]wholesome
Holy+is+magic]holistic halo+hollow]hallowed holy+day]holiday
of East+stir]Easter.

It's a start arise+is]Aries Gods+fate]gate, a sacred phase
future+date]fate of golden dawn day+lights]delights when
pass+shown]passion pass+quest)pasque+al]Pasqual flower
blooms near Passover when sun passes over equator equal day
light at preceed+recession]precession
of.equal+night/not/nox]equinox.

The repeat+(in+require+be]inquiry)+essence]request, is
query+essential)quest+on]question of the yes+sense]essence.
Astarte, Ostara, Ishtar, priestess's see East est/is where the
precious+essence]presence pleasing+essence]pleasant of
assent when spring+twigs]sprigs
spring+flung)sprung+out]sprout. It is an expected specter, a
spectacular spectator spectacle of sparkling spectrum of

spring+lights)sprites+spew+hit)spit]sprits,
spraying+twinkling]sprinkling, spreading, by
sprout+ray)spray+out]spout spores like spice+freckles]speckles
of pollen.
The
energy+stir+generation)Estrogen+repeat]Easter/East+(stop+far)
star]Easter's astronomy a+star+x]asterix rising is best
bliss+essence+did]blessed estrogen essence that is
essence+it+special]essential to the estuary.

Look at+seek]ask, see+peek]seek the see+been]seen scenic
scene+area+be]scenery see+essence]sense unseen obscene
scene+narrow]scenario!
Solar+celebrate+shown]Solabration celebrity
Shamash/Shamesh+man]Shaman sees Om Shanti sun
shine+seen]sheen and
shine+made)shade+(shine+know)shows]shadows. It's the
fall+shade]fade arrow is agnostic gnostic gnosis of the gnome
know+name+on]gnomon. So, know nom means name in
onomatopoeia. Also note+i+see]notice known notable name in
nomenclature of Astro+namer]astronomer, misnomer, anomaly
and anonymous. Like a meter+name]metronome the gnomon
points and shows nodes hours mirrored at N0+On]N0On.
S+O)sow+out+theos/theta)South+turn]southern Sun where it is
summit+realized]summarized at the summit+repeat]Summer
summons of the solstice.
Repeat+Surya+erect]resurrects and aligns to sublime
line+light]limelight of same fame name surname Surya, Sunya,
Sun-Ra's
Sow+under/See+one)Son/sun+hole/whole]soul/Sol+star]Solar
name Sol+om+on]Solomon. It's an isolated sacred+
fire]sapphire symbol of honorable+best]honest
caring+share+at+thee]charity.
The infinite Sun light outer outside iris, incites inner+sight]Insights
in infinite inner infinity. Now all one in your mind finally find, Son
light in the inner+sides]insides.

Earthwise eyes know, **Sun+wis**dom]Sunwise sun under Clock-wise circle drawn to your eyes is seen counter-clockwise to my eyes. Some say Sundaland is where **Sum**mer+**Aryans**]Sumerians came from.

The SUN Sol, **sou**th+fo**rce**(**source**+**seer**]sorcerer, sees gnomon shadow and consolidate solution to solidify all solitary soldiers of the solar nation. **Salu**te+ma**k**e+**shown**]salutation for the absolute assigned signal insignia S sine wave design for a multicultural **solar**+cele**bration**]Solabration for the sun yellow yoke yoga sun union Sol summer sault start, stay, stop, stand still, Solstice. Be consoled, with a **count**+**Sol**]council **re**peat+**solve**)reso**l**ve+solution]resolution for concealed Sun, to again sit in **Sun+day**]Sunday. In solitary **sol**emn+a**ttitude**]solitude soliloquy, seek, seeing, solicition to dissolve Son into Sun.

Time of **har**mony+(food+eat)**feed**+**st**op)**feast**]harvest is a **corn**+**you**+**copi**ous]cornucopia **feed**+**eat**+**st**op)**feast**+**i**+**ha**ve)**festi**ve+**all**]festival **feed**+**sta**y]fiesta when leaves **fail**+**all**]fall. For **carni**vore+**festival**]carnival is to devour sweet **yum**+**eat**]meat reincarnated deceased beaten beef beast. The **cut**+**leaver**]cleaver cleverly severely severs and s**lide**+**diced**]slices the s**lippery**+**liver**]slivers. Remember, rotten and red **ra**re+**thaw**]raw is wrong.

Be+**aware**]beware, be warned, be weary, of whether to worry while **W**est **w**atery **wet**+**there**]weather, and winding wild wing winds of white **win**d+**turn**]Winter wildly whip, through window and whine.

The withered widow **wet**+**seeps**]weeps, leaks and **seeps**+**wet**]sweats in her sweater as she sips the divine **vine**+**age**]vintage wine of time. She **wish**+**vesper**]whispers says sage **praise**+**air**]prayers winning winsome want wishes and waves her witch wand in west wind and verbalizes vortex verses as **invest**+**ment**al]investments of Vesta.

Dear deer, now+ear]near head+ears)hear+lead]heed heralded
chant+hear]cheer, lewd+hear]leers, and judge+hear]jeers.
Be forward+warned]forewarned further future
fin+is+shown)finish+all)final+see]finale is fine line of infinity.
Finish+near]fear fosters fate+theos]faith for our
far+(day+at+make)date/gate)fate+all)fatal+it+be]fatality.

Food Earth Farm of Grandmother Gaia

Chief chef is nice nurse **nature+real]**natural that
nourishes**+sure**ly]nurtures us with nectarines and
nut+tree+(delicate**+see)**delicacy**+lick+is)**delic**ious]**nutritious
deli+light+full]delightful **nutr**ient**+shown]**nutrition dishes of
find/**food+wish]**fish for fires fuel.

She reveals filling**+yield]**fields that build big deal meals as healing
shields and not a **dead+des**sert**ed]**desert. The
fortune**+make]**fortunate, find **fare+fee]**free fair fresh fruit, and
flower+savor+full]]flavorful flower+nou**rishing]**flourishing Florida
flora, flaunted fauna foliage or find**+down]**found
grain**+fine)gr**ind**+d**own]ground to pound down to flour.

Bow before bright brilliant **bon**d**+fire]**bonfire,
heat**+earth)**hearth**+art]**heart.
 Be show,bestow **beauty+full]**beautiful bouquets and
bounty+full]bountiful boughs with bows.

Slide**+h**urry**)s**lurry**+juice]**sluice of **c**offee**+fien**d]caffeine at the
café+interior]cafeteria and **eat+able]**edible rolling**+t**oast]roasted
toast. Then fill**+h**ole]full of **bow+hole]**bowl with
break+fasten]breakfast fuel.

Finish**+fast]**first then have a bunch of breakfast**+lunch]**brunch
with punch, then fill your paunch with too much
cracker**+munchy]**crunchy lunch.

Then find **flaccid+ab**domen)**flab+(full+at+be)**fatty]flabby,
flow+sl**oppy]**floppy fat in **glut+in]**glutton go+out]gut and
bulge**+out]**butt. Then become **obscur+scene]**obscene obese
obtuse **s**low+(**ball+loony)**balloon**+ob**long)**blob]**slob.
Then **swale+allow]**swallow glue**+in)**gluten**+chewy]**gooey
skootch**+soup]**scoops of steeped**+cream)**steam**+brew]**stew and
become **fat+sat**isfied]fatisfied. Then **spit+stew]**spew the pew ewy

broth+stew]brew. With lip+suck]licking he sucks+lips]sips, slurps and chirps then change+turns]churns and burst+ups]burps.

If you have a stick+out)stout+pudgy]stodgy stomach and you smolther+choke]smoke, it leads to struggle+stuck]struck with strong+theos]strength strangling+choke]stroke.

If you sit+led]settled in seat+dent+make)sedate+very]sedentary sit+you+make+shown]situation sedated on sedatives and submerse+glued]subdued and restrained with strong+pain]strain of spread+pain]sprain, then the stage coach stops and you are in stay+able]stable stay+shown]station stall that is stable, steady and stationary. It is a strong+wrap)strap+reign)strain+saddle]straddled sad saddle.

In stern, strict district, strike, stop staying stroll+away]stray away from straight streamlined frustrating strut+glide)stride+roll)stroll+feet]street. Then destruct, reconstruct inner+structure+shown]instruction sheet.

Then nest, rest+store)restore+act]restaurant, salivate for salad with pasty pastry pesto pasta, and a super scoop of soup for supper and finish fine dine dinner with very choke+berry]cherry fine+right]ripe vine+age]vintage wine.

Later have crazed craving sneak+act)snack at+axe]attack on bread+grain]bran cracked crackers and make become+caked]baked crumbling crumpet sugary+eat]sweet cooked+eats]cookies treats.

Gratitude+satisfied]gratified great grey grand+mother]Grandma grants conscious+gratitude+(elevate+make)elated+shown]congratulation for grade+you+make+shown]graduation to grace+show+us]gracious great+full)grateful+attitude]gratitude instead of bad+attitude]baditude. She grace+full+see]gracefully guides grandchildren to glow+over+be)glory+find]glorify glow+be)glee+had]glad to see the sunbeam's glow+stream]gleam like, queen of the serene, good glow+amorous]glamorous glow+splendid]Glenda whose

glow+fl**aring**]glaring **gl**ass+g**aze**]glaze **gl**ow+l**itters**]glitters and glistens galore.

With valor and **gra**ve+**vital**+i**s**]gravitas, she unlocks the **go**+a**ll**]goal to guard with **good**+**olden**]golden **gr**id+g**ate**]grate, the regarded Great Grandmother **Gaia's** **geo**de+**ology**)**geo**logy+gr**aph**+s**ee**]geography of Gods Garden of Eden/Garden of Eatin/In-a-gada-da-vida. There, **vibr**ate+**act**)**vibr**ant+gr**acious**]vivacious vividly variable varieties of very valuable **vege**table+**agrarian**]vegetarian **vital**+l**ittles**]vittles with **vital**+**min**imum**s**]vitamins. So valuably **re**new+**vital**+l**ive**]revive, **thr**ough+l**ive**]thrive, **sur**face+**vital**+l**ive**]survive to live and stop the vitriol of **st**op+v**irility**]sterility to revive with vim and vigor to **fu**ture+v**irility**]fertility.

See the **green**+**go**]grow and **re**peating+d**ead**)red+**st**op]rest **re**d+dust]rust. It's the salty sea seasonings of the four seasons. The aqueduct brings aquamarine water from the aquifer for **a**+**grow**+**culture**]agriculture and the **aqua**tic+**agrarian**)**aqua**rian+r**oom**]aquarium and it grows the **farm**+**and**+s**eeds**]pharmacy, a **green**+l**ow**)**grow**+**circle**+s**ee**]grocery/**green**+s**ow**)**grow**+(**source**+s**ee**)sorc**ery**]grocery.

Plea+l**ead**]plead to **up**+**ease**]appease and **up**+h**eal**]appeal for peace. **Extra**+s**peak**+**plain**]explain the **plea**+**allege**]pledge plan for the land of **plant**+**net**work]planet is to **p**ush+**lunge**]plunge **plow**+**under**]plunder and **place**+**at**]plant on plains **plat**+tabl**eau**]plateaus and **sp**ot+**places**]spaces and **di**stribute+**place**]display **pl**ot+s**paces**]places with **plea**+**ease**)**ple**ase+m**any**]plenty of **pl**ums+p**ump**)**plump**+**kin**ds]pumpkins.

So **sh**ove+t**oe**]shoe **cl**eave+h**oove**]cloven **hoof**+gr**oove**]hoove and **sh**oe+gr**oove**)**shove**+h**ole**]shovel **area**+**round**]around with **sh**ove+(**hole**+t**oe**)**hoe**]shoe in the **grow**+d**own**]ground. See the

wee **wild+seeds**]weeds in woods of the
wilder+repeat+essence}wilderness then **s**ew+**low**]sow in sod soil
with **to**+**hold**)**tool**/til+**soil**]toil. Then repeat+**low**]row like a
rake+**keep**)**reap**+repeat**er**]reaper raper taker. **M**ash+**low**]mow the
growing **we**+**eat**]wheat for **food**+**eat**+**did**]feed feast. Then hold,
hoard, graze and gorge on gorgeous greens **f**ind+**down**]found
dug deep in the **g**row+**down**]ground.

Or **for**+**rest**)**for**est+**gorg**ed]forage for fundamental fun for us
fungus near the mountain fountain or **for**est+**scav**age]forage in
smoke+**foggy**]smoggy **s**oaked+**boggy**]soggy clogged water
logged logs for frogs. Or find **fly**+**low**]flow **fl**utter+**puffy**]fluffy
fly+(**close**+**slap**)cl**apping**]flapping flocks as they **fly**+**flee**]flea in
fly+**height**]flight.

Hear their **sh**out+creak)**sh**riek+**squeal**]shrill
squeal+creak)**squ**eaks of **fl**ow+**high**)**fl**ying+**owl**]fowl owls and
scream+spe**ech**)**scr**eech+**talk**]squawk, **m**irror+**talk**]mock of
high+**cock**]hawk.
Listen to the cry of crow **ea**st+**gull**]eagle and gulls call caw.
Call+**talk**]cock-a-doodle-do rousing **rous**t+**stir**]roosters roost in
their pens with **cl**uck+**hutch**]clutch of
chick+**burp**)**ch**irp+**peep**]cheep/**chick**+**peep**]cheep and sweetly
tweet **chick**+**wrens**]chickens/**chick**+**kin**]chickens and quick click
quip+cl**ack**]quack **d**owny+**dunk**]ducks.

A stuffy **suff**er+**o**+**making**]suffocating disgusting stagnant stale
distinct **st**ink+**trench**)**st**ench+**dank**]stank of no thank
stench+**funk**]stunk like a skunk.

Middle Magic Mandala Merlin
Go clean, redeem and **day**+**dream**]daydream in the steamy
gleaming stream in middle model of prisms pristine unseen in
between. It is there that go between **medium**+**see**+**in**]medicine
men **medium**+**take**]meditate with moving mood mudras and
Mandelbrot mandala mind tools to manifest Manitou mantras for

answers. The **medic**ine+m**a**ke)**medicate**+**sh**own]medication is at the medium mid diem mid-day meridian where mediators **men**d+we**ld**)**mel**d+sme**lt**]melt, hold+m**eld**]held hoard. So, **med**ium+fi**ddle**]meddle in the **mid**+ho**le**]middle of mental meaning. Then mine mighty Midas good "golden mean" Phi, in **me**+i)**my**+end]mind/**my**+**id**)**mid**+**in**ner+**Id**e]mind third eye/I. It is the **Id**e+r**eal**]ideal **Ide**s+**ology**]ideology of **my**+**id**)**mid**+ho**le**)**middle**+one/**ine**]mine. A gay grey middle not black or white or male or female. A **mid**+**st**op]midst of history's eluding **elus**ive+**in**+i+**am**]Eleusinian **mist**+**story**]mystery that mixes **a**lloy+(**chem**ical+**mystery**)**chemi**stry]alchemy's sublime.

Store+bel**ow**]stow bestow this **store**+**see**)**stor**y+**cage**]storage of **g**low+**story**]glory. It's a **mist**+**theos**)**myth**+**magic**)**mythic**+**all**)**myth**ical+**story**]mystery/ **mist**+(**st**op+**orate**)**store**+**see**)**story**)**mystery**+**magic**)**mystic**+**is**+**i** n]mystism **his**+**store**+**be**]history.

The major mayor manager **magi**+**connect**+**make**)+**ki**netic)**mag**netic+**anim**al+**of**+**us**]magnani -mous **magi**+**make**)**magic**+**I**+**am**]magician **physic**al+**I**+**am**]physician with automatic/automagic/automathic **image**+**i**+**make**+**sh**own]imagination is an **imagin**e+**engineer**]imagineer. The **math**+(**magi**+**calculate**)**magical**]mathematical/mathmagical/matc hmagical **math**+**mat**erial+**i**+**make**+**i**+**am**]mathematician of algebra studies algorithms logarithms. They quest, quantify, quantity found findings **find**+**integer**]finger/figure out **call**+**out**]count and **calcul**ate+**us**]calculus.
They find the form of formulas which are **con**trolled+**form**+**did**]conformed formal uniform **in**ner+(**form**+**made**+**shown**)**formation**]information for the formless, reformed and deforming forces.

Like a mizer maestro **my+stern**]mister minister
mast+steer)master+son]masons' mastership amasses a majestic
mastic masonary for mass masterpieces.

Hear+bark)hark+in]harkin of hallowed
Hail+Allah+(Jehovah/raja/Jah]Hallelujah, and holler of hello, hi,
down in the **hall+low**]holler. Say hey, **who+ray**]hooray,
who+Ra]hooRah, Aho, ho ho ho, ahoy, how and
how+doing]howdy!

What+((Head+ear)hear+did)heard]words here
head+lead)heed+bark)hark+ear)hear+all]heralding the inherited
heredity of red **rose+crux+i+am**]Rosicrucian heraldry.
Merlin was the
magi+(identy+find)identified)magnified+sent]magnificent
majestic majesty i**mage+make+i+am**]magician of
Eye/i+magi)image+in+shown]imagination. He guided King
Art+Thors]Arthurs to pull e**xcellent+caliber**]Excalibur double
edged **sw**orn+**air)swear+word**]sword with a that swings and
clean**+air/cl**ean**+ear)clear+l+find**]clarifys like p**raise+air**]prayer. It
gave **awe+some**]awesome, **aw**kward+**full**]awful, audacious
au+theos+enter+i+see]authentic cross Target letter good/
God/(gold/**AU)+**su**spicious**]auspicious+**Theos+over)thor)author**
+**write**+be]Authority to write right.
Authority similar to **Theos+over/roar)Thors+day**]Thursday
Theos+under]thunder that **shy+under**]shudders,
stop+**udder**ance]stutters and **st**orm+**h**ammer]stammers.
Defended by Lancelot's lance causing laser-like
lance+serration]lacerations and **kn**ow+**right**]knights
Temples+are]Templars fight foes with force of flowing
flying+**rag**]flags.

The TAO and Wheel

At+up+pole+all)Apollo+judge+**eyes**]apologize, yes,
apogee+**pole+low)Apollo+eyes**]apologize with

Up+raised/Ap+roused]Aroused A pointing praise hands at hallowed ap/up+pole+all]Apollo.

Dios, dia Deus, dos, deuce two, ta da!
to+date)todaytwo+(got+added)gathered]together a new noon light, and mid-night twelve twirls twice the hours of Horus like (two+inner+stop]twist of (two+wind]twine. Be+twist]betwixt two+between]tween two+ones]twins of two+light]twilight twice+squeezed]tweezed and in+(twist+wind)twine)entwined+sister]twister in+near)inner+twined]intertwined, like tweed of Tweedle Dee and Tweedle Dum opposite D sides of circle are one.

The T/cross+(Above prayer hands)+Oll/all]TAO yin yang symbol comes from the sun solar shadow of the gnomon measured throughout the year. The Yin Yang in 3D.
Y+(energy+eSSence]Yes, the letter S in eSSence is the whole holy hole unity spiral circle around
S+(ball+stance)balance]symbol is designated significant sign+all]signal sign+nature]signature, galaxies. Balance TAO yin yang Father/pater+arch)patriarch+hypnotic]patriotic Mother/matter+arch)matriarch+hypnotic]matriotic mature. This Tao divided+line/one]divine dive+ides)divides+i+have]divisive determine+sides)decides+i+have]decisive dive+side)divide+(visible+shown)vision]division of divide+ends]dividends of dual+(real+it+be)reality]duality of time and sign.

Between two sides of yin yang divide hide+burrow+makes]hibernates hid+ides)hides+in]hidden invisible in I+not+divide+you+all]Individuals at mid in+near]inner down+(in+side)incise+shown)incision]decision, the He+r)her+him)herm+Aphrodite]hermaphrodite. It is a hermit+medically]hermetically cemented and sealed like a ceiling. It is like an ancient Roman a herm, a gnomon property boundary marker.

Like a **neuter+all)neutral)+eyes**]neutralized eunuch and unique the Hermetic sealed middle is **true+theos**]truth in South, North, for**th** and Tho**th**. It is Hermes **thrice+magestic+is**]Trimegitist, symbol, 3 dimensions 6 directions of N and S, E and W and Up and down that directs us, perfects us to inspect the intersection of our **per**sonal+**spect**acle+i+ha**ve**]perspective. To see Infinite dimensions of infinitemegatis God or TAO.of always NOW.

The sooner you look-see-find nature's divine design, the Temple of time and enter center in your mid **my+eye+mid**]mind, the sooner we Live in heart+**mon**o+be]harmony with**Theos Theta**'s will, the breath- death wheel, the sooner we will he**lp+all**]heal. So be aware, share, care, play fair, and pay the fair fare of the thorofare while there. The moving wheel of will is a round **r**epeating+(**win**d+flying)**wing**]ring. A reported repeating repetition, not refuted disputed is **reput**ed+m**a**de+**sh**own]reputation until **w**illed+a**way**]wanes and is **de**ad+**d**one]did. At the end of words did is ed.

The alone **cr**owned+own]crone found that the **corona**+m**a**ke+**sh**own]coronation king+**round**]crown, is a chromatic coronet, of colorful 12 chakra circles that reflects **re**calls+**lectures**]recollections like a **kolo**/*kolid*a+**siding**]colliding collage kaleidoscope.

It is AT/cross+All/**Orb**+**at**]orbit ⊕ that's **corr**alated+**right**]corrected **per+fact+did**]perfected symbol of the 4 **cards**+orig**inal**]cardinal **direct+sh**own]directions. The cross is a symbolic **sw**ear+**w**ord]sword and sun in center of round stable table a **ye**ar+whee**l**]yule log 365 call out calendar and **clap+crack**)clack **cl**ap+**tic**)**cl**ick+**tock**]clock ⊕ . It is used to **what+ch**ange]watch Theta time talk. It could be fixed by exercising, exorcizing, wee weak Xenophobes, excess fixation fears by correcting to a six day week with 5 whirling world holidays.

The years has 4 directions returning

quart+**tur**n]quarter/chaar+raji)chateraji/corners in a ⊕ rbit circle =(360days +2 solstices+2 equinoxes +1 end] 365 days of the year. There are 52 weeks/cards in a deck plus a cycle end wild card jack frost joker fool that(**Jack**+**up**+]jump t**ravel**+**jump**]trumps, **try**+**hump**]triumphs begins the new journey of the next cycle year orbit. The other joker represents the ¼ leap day every 4 years.

So above, So below reveals 3D six dimension complex vexing hexagon asterisk *"**hag**+**gal**)Hagal+**X**]hex mother rune. It's an intersect **ax**is+**hole**]axel of abraxas, that directs us to the 7th inner center axiom as a practical+**stop**]practice/ praxis.

AT+**Oll**/all] ⊕ **Theta**+**eos**/GOD is the whole hole/Holy
S+**hole**]soul a hopeful heal all hermetic
Herm+metr**opolis**]Hermopolis home of Hermes
tri+**mega**+**tis**]Trimegatis of triple thrice **three**-**fold**]trefoil treasure. THOTH/(9)
Th+**0T**/theta+ot+theta)thought+**link**)think+**knot**]thought
t**alk**+**thought**]taught, t**alk**+**reach**]teach All and
no+**ot**)not+**thing**]nothing/**no**+ ⊕Theta+**ring**]nothing.

Accurate **acro**stic+**name**]acronym N+0)N0+(0+T]0T, a ⊕cross marks the **sp**ot+p**lace**]space.
N0+**0t**/aught]not no+**aught**+**lay**]naughty nigh no+**light**]night
Know+**0t**/aught)knot+s**hows**)knows+**is**]gnosis know+**true**]knew
conscious+**knit**+**shown**]connection.
So the know/**nose**+**see**]nosy, **note**worthy+**noble**]notable
know+**able**]knowable know+**logos**]knowledge/owl
knit+th**ought**)knot+(shine+**how**)show)known+all**ege**)knowledge
+**able**]knowledgable of logged **wise**+**dome**]wisdom
act+**knowledge**)acknowledge+**head**]nodd know+**logic**+**in**]noggin.
They see through+**through**+**be**]thoroughly **true**+**stop**+**full**]trustful
true+**theos**]truth.

Don't have contempt for
con**scious**+(temper+make)**template**)**contemplat**e+**shown**]conte
mplation between temples of tempest temptations in mind. Learn

temper+**dance**]temperance of the tempo of impermanence of ⊕
Theta **G**ood+**awe**+good)God/**G**ood+**odd**]God Theos, who shows
template of **pro**vide+**tent**]protected tipi and
tent+**pole**]temple/**time**+**pole**]temples for temporary tenants
tent+apart**ments**]tenements. It is the **T**emple of **T**ime.
The **theos**+(**philo**+**sop**histry)philo**sophical**]theosophical

theism+st**ory**)theory **sh**ines+**nodes**]shows that the ⊕ thesis fact
is like a theatrical theater area arena act. **Theo**s means "with
God" found **In**+**Theos**+**use**)en**thus**ed+**i**+**am**]enthusiasm, and
names **Theo**s+(**a**+deer+**able**)ador**able**]**Theodor**, and
ad**or**+**of**+**Theos**+**thee**]Dorothy.
Theta **Theo**s+**logi**cal+**see**]theology means "God knowledge"
found also in words **th**is, **th**at, **th**en, **th**ere mon**th**s, four**th**s etc.etc.
*see chapter on letter **T***
I/eye+**at**)it+(**I**/eye+**see**)**is**]tis **the**+**is**]this/tit for **the**re+**at**]that/tat.
At+**Aten**)**at**tend+**shown**]attention, **the**+**he**)**thee**+**end**]then,
why+**end**]when, and **wh**at+)**the**+**here**)**the**re]where. It is
everywhere!

Travel and Carry

Travel+**ped**]tripping pedestrians with pedometers on pedicured
toes also pedal on **ped**+**on**+**st**ool]pedestals bikes. Some
try+**pounce**]trounce and **try**+(travel+**jump**]trump
triumph+(**attra**ctive+**beauty**)attri**bute**]tribute **tramp**+**full**]trample.
Some heard triumphant trumpery trumpets tout to troops that that
con**scious**+**tributed**]contributed to
trials+**you**+make+**shown**]tribulations.
With **trip**+**i**+**made**+**shown**]trepidation, they tried treading, trotting
on terra firma territory. They **st**ay+cl**omp**)**st**omp+**tramp**]stamped
and **tra**vel+hi**ke**)**tre**k+**stamp**]tramped. They
traipsed+**past**]trespassed and traversed leaving lasting
travel+**mark**]tracks. He **sl**ide+**trip**]slipped, **fl**y+**trip**]flipped, and
feign+qu**aint**]faint, fall, fell, frail on the terrestrial treed trail.

The mail **travel+buck**board]truck tows the trailing **tray**+follow**er**]trailer sailing on the trail and the **travel+rolly**]trolly on **pair+like+rail**)parallel roll+trail]rail **trail+back**)track. **Try+fail**]travailing travesty trials controls **travel+(take+roll)toll**]troll t**a**ke+**rifle/rip**]tariffs by finding and fining t**ire+beds**]treads **of** t**r**avel+**affect**]traffic. The ride **g**uide+**slide**]glides on a **rut**ted+**out**]route are like a root or **rut**+un**der**]rudder that follows in the **g**uide+**rudder**]gutter.

The transactions **for tran**sfer+**port**+make+**shown**]transportation on trams and train travel transferred, transformed and **trans**fer+**send**]transcended into a fast pace chase space race! So enter at+un**der**+hol**e**]tunnel carport and **put+ark**]park in **trans**fer+**port**)trans**port**+hol**es**]portal spots. Ponder important exported portmanteaus of **open+port+unity**]opportunity until **shore+lay**]surely on shore.

.

Magesty+**I**]Magi+make]magic **carry+pad+it**]carpets to c**urry+ferry**)**carry+arc**)**cart**s+**on**]carton for **chair+arc**]chariots and **car+go**]cargo **carry+c**age)**carri**age+**van**]caravans. That came to carnival carrousels, conveying **crib+bed**)+**gate**]crates and **cont**ent+re**tainer**]containers of crap arriving. They drive and drove in droves thru **deter+turn**]detours. Now we park in garages guarding gear and **gar**bled+**bag**+ing**age**]garbage.

Evolution of Man

Exhumed from **humid+moss**)**hu**mus+**man**]Human, of **human+i+be**]humanity starts **hum**ble+**little+made**]humiliated as a **hum**ble+frag**ility**]humility of a homunculi. He knows nada nothing and is a naked nomad **not+evil**]naïve, a **nat**ural+**live**]native, **kn**own+s**lave**]knave of a **nat**ure+**shown**]nation. **Gene**+gno**sis**]genesis/**genes**+of+**Isis**]genesis generated **Indi**vidual+**genesis**]indigenous natives. Genitalia generates genetic gender gestated congenital genes **re**peat+**generating**]regenerating into **gen**e+**era**+make+**shown**]generations.

Then with **add+it+sh**own]addition of Adam's apple. Adam

became **many+men)man+be]**manly menacing men manually **comm**ent+de**mand]**commanding with manifestos, manifesting **man+i+pol**itical+**made+shown]**manipulation and **man+**cage)**manage+ment**al]**managment with manuals of **man+overing]**manuvering **man+d**omin**ate]**mandates.

See the **djin+in+us]genius** is an (**in**ner+(**gene+be**)genie)**ingen**ious+**seer]**engineer with **in+gen**ie+**you+be]**ingenuity. Perhaps they become generals or generous **gen**tle+subtle)**gentle+man]**gentlemen or generally generic **gent+vile]**gentiles or the geriatric gentry.

The race of races are like classes to pass that classified castle class, or caste systems that are **cloist**er+**tro**pic+**phobic]**claustrophobic and **col**lide+(**close+asp**)cl**apsed]**collapsed. They **close+wrench]**clench, **close+pinch]**clinch, **line+pinch]**lynch like a clothes line in a **cloth+thos**e)**clothes+it]**closet.

A catapulted **cos**mos+mag**ic)**cosmic **comes+it]**comet causes and catalyzes **cata**clysm+**tropic]**catastrophic categorical chaos. Star/**aster+void]**asteroid casts castrating paranoid fear of void to avoid risky **down+**(**aster+x**)**asterisk]**disaster. Its an epic epoch Up/**appo**lo+e**clipse]**apocalypse collapse, with **down+b**astard+**be]**dastardly, **dam**ned+**aged+ring]**damaging, damming, **con**scious+**deemed]**condemned **aft+re**peat)**after+math]**aftermath/actual math.

The **sheep+herd**er]shepherd with **staff+pasture]**stature is a **past+store]**pastor who **shave+near]**shears the **gold+in]**golden fleece. He **find+holes]**fools the **follow+lock]**flock of **shee**p+**people]**sheeple fooled fold at the **steep+**(**tent+pole**)**temple]**steeple. With **fright+hear/near/tear)fear+regret)**fret of the white lightening Thor+**under]**thunder he cheers of dove true love above **light+**(**warn+heard**)**word]**lord. Then he hypnotizes and **Bapt**ist+**eyes]**baptizes in bubbling babbling born again **bath+is+I+am]**baptism. Then the **mind+I+stir]**minister/(**mind+I+store]mini**sters+**strol**ling)minstrals administer and undermine and mines **my+**end]mind of mine. The **parish+partition]**parishioners, partake and participate in passing past **purge+story]**purgatory and proceed to rap trap rhapsody for **wrap+capture**]rapture to prepare for parting departure party with particular pariah **Messiah.** Who after departed, others imparted a messy mass message at masses that has been used for an abuse excuse for **mass+occures**]massacres.

Nuns with nothing inhabit in **hat+bit**]habits/hajab have good God haughty **habits+at**]habitats. Some **previous+intending**]pretending raising, praying prestigious priests put on prayformance, playformance, **perfect+form+dance**]performance for you. Some **sw**inging+l**ay)sway+wiggle**]swiggle **swine+handle**]swindle. Some have preferences, **previous+tense**]pretenses, **pray+reachers**]preachers prowling for precious prey. With cunning, conning, converting, confiding, confessing, confining they control **control+vers**e+i+al**l**]controversial confessionals. **Cathartic+theos+holy+make**]catholic from the **cat**hedral **cata**gory+tomb]catacomb caches its **cat+chase**]catch of cash, that can be traded, stashed and can crash in a flash or turn to ash. Those standing in the **discip**le+line]discipline **don**or+make]donates some sum of dough/money to **buy+got**]bought, the not to be sailed/**sell+old**]sold, the **hold+cleave)heave+very**]heavy, cold, solid gold. It is this treasure they hardily **have+old)**]hold+hard]hoard. But the **mouse+voles**]moles in **kn**ob+hole]knolls know for sure they boldly store more with whole full **bow**ed+hole]bowls.

Marriage to Birth

Her bustier **boosted+oblong**]boob balls, **bump+utter**]butter **round+bust**]robust **Bring+est**rogen]Beasts busting bursting out like her bustle on her **Bum bulge+out**]butt **high+bump**]hump. When the virtuous vestal **vortex+*urge*+in+**]virgin hail Mary is to be married. She is going **stay+ready**]steady with **care+rage**]courage to **care+fully**]carefully care for the **carry+age**]carriage. After she is then **marry+age/stage**]marriage for **mare**+carriage]marriage and she gets a promise **pro**vision+**pos**tion+sale]proposal. She is guided **bit+ride+led**]bridled and **halt+her+led**]haltered and **dull**ed+**d**own)dolled up and given a **bride+doll**]bridal/ **bit+ride+hold**]bridal **show+her**]shower with **sack+hold**]sachel. She is **hand+hold**]handled, **down+angled**]dangled

to be ridden and riding+angled]wrangled and
sit/sat+hold]saddled for glide horseback slow+ride]slide from
stall+is+on]stallion steed studs in a stay+able]stable stable. She
gets husband's husbandry's name brand with
bond+confining]binding we/wet+bedding]wedding band on hand.

She'll be fill+bucket]fuck it hump bumped with+life]wife, as
my+aid]maid serf like serve+nice)service+act]servant, made
slaves for sloven slobs for no my+need]money.

The punitive+crunch]punch punative+shove]pushing now power
of poke+in+to]point pen of heinous pee+in+us]penis. It
pee+enter+makes]penetrates/penial+enter+
(reap+takes)rapes]penetrates, the love+lay]lovely V cut/cunt of
the Virgo V+urge+in]virgin's vagina vulva, vulgar cave of heart
shape "eVe" goddess of low+grooVe]love V+in+us]Venus.
Venus/Lucifer fallen angel, luminous luminance
ill+lumin+not+i)illumi+Nazi+shown]illumination, is translucent
morning evening star St Lucy light.

She becomes matron+sure]mature for
matter+eternity)maternity+moan+need]matrimony of monstrous
monopolizing monolith+mental]monument groan of gambling
gambit of monotonous+game+see]monogamy in a one monk
mono+story(monastery+make]monastic money monarchy. Then
she becomes smashed+my+other)Mother+did]smothered as
she begets a human being and births be+holds]beholds
beginning, Ba breath Ba+be's]baby's body
being+comes]becomes to be into be+ring]being and is
some+body]somebody.

The Bible, has be+lie+far)belief+leaves]believes, slip+stick] slick
slid+by]sly, said+lie]sly Eve is violet even+at)event+ring]evening
is evil. Some blaming Eve burden+busting]bursting, blooming
born sore torn utter+torus]uterus
woman+room)womb+mans]woman birth. They

bleed+fl**ood**)bl**o**od+cl**ot**]blot blood+l**eading**]bleeding
blood+r**ush**]blushes bearing, bobbling, bubbling, babbling
ba+be]baby's breath. The nothing+**ot**)n**ot+final**]infant is
infinite+is+small]infinitesimal of the n**ot+final+it**]infinite. It is
I/**eye+n**)in+n**0**+sence)innocent+**see**]innocence and a
no+in)nin+see)ninny+**come**+poop]nincompoop no+it+wit]nitwit.

Mother must clean disgusting dysentery of diet+in**jest**]digested
dia**rr**hea+wiper]diaper. The **sl**ump+gl**op**]slop **pl**unge+p**op**]plop,
pew+acrid]putrid, poo+goop]poop goo juice like
brown+bl**ack**+is+sh**own)bra**ckish+wine]brine.

She must nurse, nurture and nourish with breast dip+hole]dimple
the point+d**imple**]pimple, model of **bott**om/pot+holed]bottle
nip+hole]nipple. She lapse+falls)lulls+a+baby]lullaby with lips
liking and licking lull+jolly]lolly pops.

She must person+sway+made]persuade, bounce,
swing+lay)sway+cuddle/coddle]swaddle huddle the
roll+bumble]rumble bump+juggle)bungle+fumble]bumble baby
bundle. She must stop+(fail+all)fall+bumble]fumbling)stumbling,
jump+rumble]jumbling, running, and walk+weird]awkward
teetering of the walk+(head+bobble)hobble]wobbling
tot+waddler]toddler.
The dimmed, dense, dunce+numb]dumb, thumb sucking baby
making mud+puddled]muddled
muted+utter)mutter+jumble+wing]mumbling
stop+mutter]stuttering must be tot/taught talk/thought. The
young+theos]youth must be
proclaim+loud)proud+raised]praised and taught+reached]teach
true+theos]truth.
She must talk+reach]teach until tell+ought]taught to sit+at]sat
down, shove+it]shit, poop plan+drop]plop, tough+curd]turd on
the pot.

Kids are Kindergarten **kin+hundred**]kindred kindly
kind+folk]kinfolk from connected
kin+ring)king+dome/home]kingdom of mankind. They dominate
our **furniture+finished**]furnished **dormer+story**]dormitory
condos+dome+mini+home]condominium
domicile+home)dome+nest+make]domestic
free+dome]freedom.

The challenging **changing+wild**]child puppet
puppy+(peep+holes)people]pupils in pews with open
pupa+holes]pupils. In primary
skilled+collar)scholars+fool]school they are scolded and with
prime primer, and the principal imprints
princes+estrogen]princesses with principles or they
fly+wing)fling+done)flung flounder+sunk]flunk. Then they
become **be+(twix+teen)tween**]between a
a+dull+ultimate)adult+essence]adolescents that idolize.

Then **private+league**]privilege pri**vy+league**/ivy league,
collective+league]colleagues on **collection+knowledge**]college
camp+us]campuses unifies **cival+very**]chilvary
city+them)citizen+village)civil+wized]civilized site.
Then the cycle of mating and marriage starts again and, dutiful
doting perennial parental cuddling coddling
combined+poles]couples **copy+much+be**]copiously
circle+repeating+make)create+you+are]creature
people+copulation]population.

Job Obligation to Death

Legitimate **ligurature+all**]legal system legislature **all+legara**]allege
legara is bine/tie, to leg and
repeat+leg+(captive+sure)capture)ligature+shown]religion.
Obey+do+it)obedient+be]obediently your
jack+up)Jump+(obligate+be)obey]job+ligature+make+shown]job
ligation. **Obey+(legara+capture)ligature+shown**]obligation of

in+ploy+mental]employment in energy+con+of+me]eCONomy to extra+ploy+it]exploit for profit.
Then like hobo+bit)hobbits+goblin]hobgoblin with clog+hobnail]cobbling job hobby, they hobble+noble]hobnob grovel with goblets in the lobby.

Old+timers]Alzheimer on alcohol or Tylenol are falling be+((wittle+weather)wither+melt)wilt+repeated]bewildered and fizzled shrank+drivled]shriveled are drip+bubble)dribble+falling]drooling old fools catching cool+old]colds.
Then disappointing all+ill+being]ailing diagram+gnosis+make]diagnostic point at poignant prognostic prognosis. So be telepathic and symptoms+(empath+theos+make)pathetic]sympathetic and similar+empathize)sympathy+eyes]sympathize and patiently pet apathetic patients suffering from pathogens.
For the chilled ill pilfer+rampage]pillage for pain+ill]pills and wade+low]wallow but fail to fill full their pull+well]pail and deal with real feelings. The down+well]dwell, real sweet+well]swell off fare-thee-well+theos]wealth is the fair holy great+pail]grail ale that helps heal+art]heart health.
With+elevation)well+(heal+theos)health]wealth is Hold/balance+Essence/energy+Air+light)heal+theos]Health in Theta/God or Center. .

All+lone)alone+(one+be)only]lonely long to be+long]belong and sing+on+go]song+done]sung when going+done]gone.

Yell+help]yelp for help+feeling]healings for hurt ill in host+pity+able)hospice+it+able+all]hospital+hotel]hostel or a hostess at house+my)home+motel]hotel.

Blast+flair]blare flab+(gasp+blast]flabbergasted gust when expired+gasp+(repeat+(spirit+hole)spiral+make+shown)respiration]exasperated from

gasping+res**piration**(as**piration**+**fixa**te+m**aking**)as**ph**yxiating+fau
lt)asphalt/**ass**+**fart**]asphalt.

The slow+s**oft**]sloth **s**lope+c**rouchs**]slouches on a couch and
slide+**lump**]slumps and slides+**under**]slumbers in a steep
slide+**deep**]sleep. It's like a
sl**ip/sl**ope+gu**ide/ride**)**sl**ide+**bed**]sled+**lay**]sleigh that
sl**ips**+**low**]slows to dying+b**ed**]dead/**down**+**end**]dead. Then the
down+l/eyes]dies, and the whole holy **see**+**hole**]soul,
flo**ws**+**sky**]flys to **h**eaven+**sky**]high.

Mortal+**rules**)**morals**+**l**+**see**]morality rules mortal man. He is
caged to make wages for amortized **mort**al+en**gage**]mortgage
until **repeatedly**+**tired**]retired til **mort**al+**finality**]mortality of death.
The mortified mourn with **re**membered+**morose**]remorse the rigor
mortis at the mortician's **hor**ror+**bad**]horrid **mort**al+**bad**]morbid
mortuary.

I rays+**rise**]**raise** eye to **h**eaven+**i**)**hig**h+sight]height
at+**seek**]**ask**+**why**]sky.

We all take our **ch**ange+**turn**]churn in this **so**lo+**journ**ey]sojourn
to return and adjourn to earnestly **l**et+**earn**]learn our center
internal **etern**al+(**I**+**not**+**fin**ish+**see**)infin**ity**]eternity.

For all **cr**awl+**leap**)**cre**ep+**critters**]creatures of
create+ma**ke**+**shown**]creation leads to crematory remains of
circle+repeat+yum)**cream**+**make**+**shown**]cremation that are
burned, churned, and interned in urn for eternity. Some are
disemboweled embalmed, hurry buried in
glowing+(**die**+g**round**)**d**own+l**oom**)d**oom**]gloom of deep depth of
done+br**eath**]death honeycomb catacomb tomb/room.

The dark **d**one+**i**)**die**+eat]diet/**don't**+**eat**]diet lead to
dis+**ease**+**did**]diseased **d**own+**cease**]deceased.
See **dust**+**see**]destiny is

down+I)die+did)dead+theos)death+essence+stop+in+see]desti
ny in the distant+stance]distance. It is the destitute, destroyed,
deteriorating, decay, decomposed, dust+dark]dusk, rot. It is the
red+muddy]ruddy, red+dusty]rusty, rustic,
molecule+old)mold+dew]mildew, the mold+dusty]musty mulch,
dread+down]drown+lousy]drowsy to
deep+(down/dirt+earth)depth]death down+end]dead.

Ex+cave+make]excavate
in+(groove+cave)grave+dead]engraved cave+gravity]cavity
ground+cave)grave+(cave+it+be)cavity]gravity.It is the
under+taker]undertaker who takes you under.
Epic+(faint+one)phantom+see]epiphany
epic+summarize]epitomize epic+dialogue]epilogue of
epic+graph]epitaph with an orbit+you+are+see]obituary for
obliterate+live+beyond]oblivion.

Telate+i+haves]relatives
memory+I+all)memorials+eyes]memorialize and
remind+is+nice]reminisce remorsefully with
memory+eyes]memorized remain+acts]remnants of
rewind/repeat+mind)remind+memory+buried]remembered in
my+in)mine+end]mind's eye.
The pun is of the funding a
fun+fer+all]funeral/fume+hole]fumerole furnace function is a
foundation+mental]fundamental family
connect+(jump+connection)junction]conjunction.

This is when we contemplate the
be+lack)black+mind)blind+wink]blink, twice+blink+little]twinkle,
blind+leery)bleary+furry]blurry, blend+hue)blue+weak]bleak,
blah+say]blasé, blank+sand]bland blindfold of light and death.

We wander+ponder)wonder pontificate about
being+yonder]beyond, passing on, and long longing to belong
and sing the solum sung song of when going gone.

103

We follow and find fine line of time **to+goes**)tows+**ward**]toward **to**+(**more**+**dawn**ing)**mor**ning+**O**/all]tomorrow **on+ward**]onward **fro+come**]from of **be+for**mer]before. Therefore **fly+go**]flow forthright **forth+toward**]forward for **four+ten**)fourteen+**night**]fortnight.

With **fort**+**attitude**]fortitude fortify **a+for**ward]afford **fort**une+**you+make**]fortunate future forces. Find and file findings **pro**fit+**found**]profound. **Inner+form+made+shown**]information of **inner+nova+shown**]innovation is **new+views**)news+**over+above**)nova+**all**)novel+**be**]novelty.

From zero to zygote, to zombie zap dead end, from protozoa to **zoo+ark**]zodiac, Zion, to **Zen**+i+**theta**]zenith of Deus/Zeus. There see zealous Zoroaster's **Z**ed+**million**]zillion stars, and zipping zephyrs, return to Zeptepi!.

For **magi+ma**ke)magic majesty Omega's megalithic megaphone magnifies the magnitude of magnificent, ominously hum oms Aum omitted omen poem. That honing cloned drones and omnipotent ohm computer coming home. A detective detects protecting of defective product technologic dynamic dynamite dynamo **robot**+**magic**]robotic being created creates robot beings. So I will close the, the curtains and curtly **cut+tale**]curttail and close this **curio+sit+see**]curiosity cabinet, and the cute, curious, current court courtesan will courteously curtsie.

Post+you+**make**]postulate at the **oppose+it+shown**/**oppos**ing+**sights**]opposition because **wreck+less**]reckless wrecks more and **not+valuable**])invaluable, it is more valuable.
Because **hyper+pose+thesis**)hypothesis)**it+all**]hypothetical in **parent+thesis**]parenthesis **is** place+**cause+possible**]plausible and **pro**be+**able**]probable proof of **pro**be+**blame**)**problem**+**agress**]progress that has probility of the synopsis synthesis.

Synopsis synthesis: This Author believes that many word sound fragments are connected to other words. Unfortunatley this theory is not provable through traditional facts of linguistics and that is why the word Lany**myth**ic contains the word "myth". However, this Art of Thor Author believes that a 3D mindmap model of how word fragments are connected could and will be developed using fragmathic Langmythic logic in the future. This will reveal a complex interconnected 3D cluster similar to how neuron connections are shown in a graphic representation of a brain.

God Now Gnowing

You don't know what you don't know. Because **Knowledge** is only knowing owning alleged legends of
repeating+**lig**ature+**l**+**on** religions.
But the Shambala shaman shade man shows now,
the shadow of the Son/Sun of Soul/Sol Om On Solomon.
It is the Theos, green growing flowing shadow in center Om,
the (**God**+**nam**es+**on**)gnomon, direct know is **Gnosis** of in
center ring; the true Gnowing. It is, I see Isis, direct
experience of 4 cards
of cardinal dire right direct shown directions of Sol stops
Solstices and even equal night Equinoxes.
It's a right story rectory that directs us and correctly relate
correlates in know in noggin by cone center making,
concentrating the conscious knitting, connect show us
consciousness on the outer crystal criss cross time pole
Temple of Time.
It is also reflected and see in seen being twisted between
in inner spiraling inspiring experience of expiring spirit.
It's between our mind temples tempering our temper by
circling entering the center to the mid in find of mind the eye
of the I. The Hermit sees the hid in hidden her him hermetic
seal middle,

it's the medicine medication found in medium made shown meditation. It is where we find I magi images of inner magic make shown imagination and inner not final infinity, inside and out.

Letter-Multiplication Table

A	B	C	D	E
A At Above	AB -Not Normal	AC-Before	AD Add	AE
BA Breath	BB Burst Bi	BC	BD BAD	BE
CA	CB	CC Circular	CD	CE~See
DA	DB	DC	DD Down	DE - Undo
EA Early	EB	EC	ED did	EE Energy
FA Far	FB	FC	FD FOUND	FE
GA	GB	GC	GD GOD	GE Gaia Gee-right
HA Haw Left	HB	HC	HD	HE
IA	IB	IC	ID	IE
JA jack	JB	JC	JD	JE ject
KA	KB	KC	KD	KE Key
LA	LB	LC	LD	LE hold Ball
MA Mother Matter	MB	MC	MD	ME
NA	NB	NC	ND NOD	NE
OA	OB Oblong Job	OC	OD~Odd	OE
PA Father	PB	PC	PD	PE Pee
QA	QB	QC	QD	QE
RA Sun	RB	RC	RD	RE-repeat
SA	SB	SC -SK Scrape	SD SOD	SE See
TA ~PTAH God of Creation	TB	TC	TD	TE
UA	UB	UC	UD	UE
VA Vagina	VB	VC	VD VID -To See	VE
WA	WB	WC	WD	WE
XA	XB	XC	XD	XE
YA	YB	YC	YD	YE The
ZA End	ZB	ZC	ZD	ZE
KEY	~ Sounds like phonetically			
Prefix	Stand alone word		COMBO letter Tendencies	
Suffix	Letter Meanig Tendendcies		Associations	

F	G	H	I	J
AF	AG	AH	AI	AJ
BF	BG	BH	BI two	BJ
CF	CG	CH CHI chop cho	CI SIGH	CJ
DF	DG	DH	DI DIE	DJ
EF	EG	EH	EI	EJ
FF Future	FG	FH	FI	FJ
GF	GG Good Glitter	GH	GI GUY	GJ
HF	HG	HH Half Hold	HI	HJ
IF	IG	IH	II Inner	IJ
JF	JG	JH	JI	JJ Joke Jump
KF	KG	KH	KI	KJ
LF	LG	LH	LI	LJ
MF	MG	MH	MI~MY	MJ
NF	NG	NH	NI	NJ
OF	OG	OH	OI	OJ
PF	PG	PH	PI	PJ
QF	QG	QH	QI	QJ
RF	RG	RH	RI Rye	RJ
SF	SG	SH Show	SI Sigh	SJ
TF	TG	TH Theta	TI Tie	TJ
UF	UG	UH	UI	UJ
VF	VG	VH	VI Victory Victim	VJ
WF	WG	WH Wonder	WI Why	WJ
XF	XG	XH	XI	XJ
YF	YG	YH	YI	YJ
ZF	ZG	ZH	ZI	ZJ

K	L	M	N	O
AK	AL All	AM	AN	AO
BK	BL Black	BM	BN	BO
CK	CL Close	CM	CN	CO
DK	DL DALE DELL DILL DOLL	DM	DN	DO
EK	EL Elevate	EM	EN	EO
FK	FL Fly Flow	FM	FN	FO
GK	GL	GM	GN = N	GO
HK	HL	HM	HN	HO~Hoe
IK	IL~ILL light and sick	IM I'M	IN	IO
JK	JL	JM	JN	JO
KK Connect Quest cho	KL Close	KM	KN = N or kin	KO
LK Lack Like Lock	LL Light Lack	LM	LN	LO
MK	ML	MM Mother	MN	MO
NK	NL	NM	NN NO	NO
OK	OL~all	OM	ON	OO Round Mouth
PK Pack Peck Pick Pick	PL	PM Post Meridian	PN	PO
QK	QL	QM	QN	QO
RK	RL	RM	RN	RO~Row
SK or X	SL Slip	SM	SN snake	SO
TK Tic Toc	TL	TM	TN	TO
UK	UL	UM	UN under	UO
VK	VL Valuable	VM	VN	VO
WK	WL	WM	WN	WO~ Woe
XK	XL	XM	XN	XO
YK	YL	YM	YN	YO
ZK	ZL	ZM	ZN	ZO

P	Q	R	S	T	U
AP up	AQ	AR air	AS	AT	AU gold author
BP	BQ	BR	BS	BT	BU
CP	CQ	CR	CS	CT	CU
DP	DQ	DR	DS	DT	DU ~Doo
EP	EQ	ER Repeat	ES essense	ET	EU
FP	FQ	FR Fear	FS	FT	FU
GP	GQ	GR Growth	GS	GT	GU~Goo
HP	HQ	HR	HS	HT	HU~Who
IP	IQ	IR	IS	IT	IU
JP	JQ	JR	JS	JT	JU~Jew jump
KP	KQ	KR	KS	KT	KU~Coo
LP	LQ	LR	LS	LT	LU
MP	MQ	MR	MS	MT	MU
NP	NQ	NR	NS	NT	NU~New
OP	OQ	OR	OS	OT OUGHT	OU
PP Power Plant Pi	PQ	PR	PS	PT	PU
QP	QQ Quest choic	QR	QS	QT	QU question KV
RP	RQ	RR Repeat	RS	RT	RU
SP SPIT out mouth	SQ	SR	SS ~es So	ST Stop	SU~S
TP	TQ	TR TRAVEL	TS	TT Theta Center	TU~Too
UP	UQ	UR	US	UT	UU Under
VP	VQ	VR	VS	VT	VU
WP	WQ	WR	WS	WT	WU
XP	XQ	XR	XS	XT	XU
YP	YQ	YR	YS Yes	YT	YU
ZP	ZQ	ZR	ZS	ZT	ZU

V	W	X	Y	Z
BV	BW	BX	BY be by	BZ
CV	CW	CX	CY~see	CZ
DV	DW	DX	DY	DZ
EV evil eve	EW goo	EX	EY	EZ
FV	FW	FX	FY	FZ
GV	GW	GX	GY~Gee	GZ
HV	HW	HX	HY~Hi	HZ
IV I have	IW	IX	IY	IZ eyes
JV	JW	JX	JY	JZ
KV	KW	KX	KY~Key	KZ
LV	LW	LX	LY~ Lee	LZ
MV	MW	MX	MY	MZ
NV	NW	NX	NY	NZ
OV	OW~O all	OX	OY	OZ
PV	PW	PX	PY	PZ
QV	QW	QX	QY	QZ
RV	RW	RX	RY	RZ
SV	SW swing	SX	SY	SR
TV	TW	TX~Tex	TY~ Tee	TR Travel
UV	UW	UX	UY	UZ
VV Victor V Shap	VW	VX	VY	VZ
WV	WW Wonder	WX	WY why	WZ wize
XV	XW	XX Intersect	XY	XZ
YV	YW	YX	YY~ I Or E See	YZ
ZV	ZW	ZX	ZY	ZZ End

Language+fract+fact+make]Langfractic
Fractal+dictionary]Fractionary
Word fragments within words added together.

A) ?	Up/Ap At Above
able+**out**) ?	about
Above+it+**gain**+**doing**) ?	obtaining
above+**see**) ?	observe
able+**brief**+de**viations**) ?	abbreviations
above+round+**change**) ?	arch
above+**vault**+**launch**) ?	avalanche
acquired+**quaint**+**stances**) ?	acquaintances
act+**shown**) ?	action of actors
action+**real**+**it**+**be**) ?	actuality
added+**mirror**+**make**+**shown**) ?	admiration
adore+**mental**) ?	adornments
accurate+**complete**+**show**+**did**)?	accomplished
act+**real**) ?	actual
add+**optical** +**shown**) ?	adoption
add+**damn**+**see**) ?	adamantly
add++(**no**+**joys**)**noise**) ?	annoy
add+**it**+**shown**) ?	addition
add+**verbs**) ?	adverbs
add+**wise**) ?	advise
admit+**shown**) ?	admission
adult+**less**+**essence**) ?	adolescent
a+**dual**+**at**+**repeat**+**of**+**us**)	adulterous
ad**vance**+**minister**+**maker**) ?	administrator
affected+**flow**+**hence**) ?	affluence
after+**math**) ?	aftermath
aged+**elder**) ?	angel
a+**grow**+**culture**) ?	agriculture
Agni+**grave**+**make**) ?	aggravates
agni+**makes**) ?	agitates
agriculture+**aryan**)?	agrarian
aim+**bit**+**shown**) ?	ambition
aim+**vision**) ?	ambition
air+**bow**) ?	arrow
air+**ones**) ?	Aryans
Al**chemy**+**mystery**) ?	chemistry

alloy+**chemis**try) ?	alchemy
all+**c**orrect) ?	OK
all+**legen**d) ?	alleged
all+**ligature+l**+stance) ?	allegiance
all+**ligature+**engage**+shown**) ?	alligation
all+**letter**+make+**shown**) ?	alliteration
all+**thee+arch+see**) ?	oligarchy
ally+**cove**) ?	alcove
Alter+make) ?	ultimate
A+**maze**+doing) ?	amazing
Amen+mend) ?	amend
amuse+mag**ic**) ?	music
a+**name+minus**) ?	anonymous
a+**noun+see**+make) ?	annunciate
anim**ated+mammal**)?	animal
ante+**agonizing**) ?	antagonizing
any+**noi**se) ?	annoy
up+**prove+all**) ?	approval
A/up+**spear**+ **g**rass) ?	asparagus
ap+**collapse**) ?	apocalypse
apex+at**titude**) ?	aptitude
appear+**at**) ?	apparent
appear+**it**+**sh**own) ?	apparitions
Ap+flu+end+za) ?	Affluenza
appo**sing+pole+sit**) ?	opposite
appo**sing+point**) ?	opponent
app**ropriate+pl**ease) ?	appease
aqua**rian**+ro**om**) ?	aquarium
aqua**tic**+agra**rian**) ?	aquarian
a+**rhythm+metric**) ?	arithmetic
are+at) **?**	art
art+**official**) ?	artificial
arc+**change+angle**) ?	archangels
arch+**air**+be) ?	archery
arch+**cover+act**) ?	arch ofthecovenant
arch**aic**+th**eology**) ?	archeology
ar**ise+is**) ?	Aries
art+**talk+you+make+shown**) ?	articulation
art+**official**) ?	artificial
area+**round**) ?	around
a+**spear+grass**) ?	asparagus
a+**swear**) ?	answer
asset+**similar+make**) ?	assimilate
as**set+social+make**) ?	associate

a+**star**+**x**) ?	asterisk
aster+**x**) ?	asterisk
aster+v**oid**) ?	asteroid
astro+**log**os) ?	astrology
a+**star**+**namer**) ?	astronomer
astrology+**name**+**see**) ?	astronomy
astronomical+**theology**) ?	astrotheology
at+**axe**) ?	attack
at+**com**mon+m**ake**) ?	accommodate
at+g**ain**) ?	attain
At+**land**+it+**is**) ?	Atlantis
At+up+**Helios**+**on**) ?	Aphelion
at+**lone**) ?	Atone
Atman+**of**+**sphere**) ?	atmosphere
Atom+make) ?	Atomic
at+**on**) ?	Aton
at+**seek**) ?	ask/axe
at**tention**+apt**itude**) ?	attitude
at+**tense**+**sh**own) ?	attention
at+**under**+h**ole**) ?	tunnel
at+**last**) ?	alas
at+**under**+h**ole**) ?	tunnel
aura+**Ra**) ?	aurora
author+**write**+**be**) ?	authority
auto+**make**) ?	automake
avatar+**alien**) ?	avian
avian+**navig**ate) ?	aviate
aviate+**re**peat) ?	aviators
x+**fact**+really) ?	exactly
x+**at**+real**ly**) ?	exactly
Axe+i+**dent**)?	accident
axe+fault) ?	assault
B) ?	**bi 2**
Ba+**be**) ?	Baby
b**ad**+**ill**) ?	bill
b**ad**+**tra**der+**all**) ?	betrayal
b**ad**+**witch**) ?	bitch
b**alance**+**all**) ?	ball
b**alance**+**dis**play) ?	ballets
ball+**dis**play) ?	ballet
balloon+**ob**long) ?	blob
ball+**loon**y) ?	balloon
ball+**stance**) ?	balance
ball+**wobble**) ?	bobble

ball+old) ? heads look like ball	bald
bandana+idi**ots**) ? **bad**+hab**its**) ?	bandits
bank+trick**ster**) ?	banksters
bad+t**alk**) ?	balk
bath+**is**+**in**) ?	baptism
beauty+**full**) ?	beautiful
be+**come**) ?	become
become+c**aked**) ?	baked
be+**essence**+**st**op) ?	best
be+**friend**) ?	befriend
be+**hide**+**find**) **?**	behind
be+**leaded**) ?	believed
belief+**i**+ha**ve**) ?	believe
bell+**jelly**) ?	belly
be+**low**) ?	below
be+**low**+**under**) ?	blunder
below+under**neath**) ?	beneath
benefitting+official) ?	beneficial
beneficial+**diction**) ?	benediction
be+not+**violent**) ?	benevolent
bent+**low**) ?	bowed
benefit+**official**) ?	beneficial
be+**trader**+**all**) ?	betrayal
be+**unity**+**full**) ?	beautiful
be+**aware**) ?	beware
Bi+**lible**) ?	Bible
bi+**look**) ?	book
bind+**are**+thee) ?	binary
bind+**ridge**) ?	bridge
biota+**log**os+**all**) ?	Biological
bisect+**take**) ?	bite
bisect+**two**) ?	bit
bite+**in**) ?	bitten
biting+**winter**) ?	bitter
bit+**ride**+**hold**) ?	bridle
black+**leery**) ?	bleary
black+**name**) ?	blamed
bliss+**essence**+**did**) ?	blessed
blizzard+**luster**) ?	bluster
blow+**dust**y) ?	blustery
blowing+ha**zz**ard) ?	blizzard
blow+qu**icks**) ?	blitz
blue+**lack**) ?	black
bobbin+w**obbling**) ?	bobbling

boil+**cake**) ?	bake
bond+**fire**) ?	bonfire
bond+**round**+be**)** ?	boundry
born+**earth**) ?	birth
bounty+**full**) ?	bountiful
bow+**end**) ?	bend
bow+**hole**) ?	bowl
brat+**other**) ?	brother
breakfast+**lunch**) ?	brunch
bread+grain) ?	bran
break+**fast**en) ?	breakfast
briar+**ramble**) ?	bramble
bride+**doll**) ?	bridal
bridled+**ride**) ?	bride
bring+**bought**) ?	brought
brother+**hotel**) ?	brothel
bulb+**ball**) ?	bubble
bubble+**oil**) ?	boil
brown+**mood**) ?	brood
bug+**flutter**+**by**) ?	butterfly flutter by
bull+**lig**ature+**relent**+see) ?	belligerently
bull+i+**close**) ?	bellicose
build+**under**) ?	bunkers
bump+**hole**) ?	bubble
buffoon+**funny**) ?	phoney
build+**under**) ?	bunker
bull+**lig**ature+**rant**) ?	belligerent
burst+**ups**) ?	burps
busy+**dizzying**) ?	buzzing
busy+**in**+**ess**ence) ?	business
buy+**got**) ?	bought
C) ?	**Conscious, Circular, Change**
circle	**circle**
café+**interior**) ?	cafeteria
calculate+**us**) ?	calculus
call+**out**) **?**	count
call+**talk**) ?	cock
calm+**passion** =?	compassion
can+g**ood**) ?	could-relate should
camp+**us**) ?	campus
carry+**far**+**at**) **?**	cart
carry+**van**) ?	caravan
care+**rage**) ?	courage
care+**repeat**+**actor**) ?	character

carnivore+festival) ?	carnival
cascade+disaster+tropic/circle?	catastrophic
capacity+able) ?	capable
cataclysm+tropic)	catastrophic
catagory+tomb) ?	catacomb
cat+chase) ?	catch
catch+got) ?	caught
caucus+Asians) ?	Caucasians
cause+make+shown) ?	causations
cause+action) ?	causation
cause+sick) ?	caustic
cave+groove) ?	cove
cave+in) ?	cavern
cavern+land+yonder) ?	canyon
cavern+vortex) ?	cavort
cathartic+theos+holy+make) ?	catholic
center+all) ?	central
certify+make) ?	certificate
chair+man) ?	chairman
change+turning) ?	churning
chi/change+stance) ?	chance
change+advance) ?	chance
change+barge) ?	charge
change+angels) ?	changels
chant+hear) ?	cheer
change+share+at+thee) ?	charity
certify+obtain+see) ?	certainly
change+racing) ?	chasing
change+reins) ?	chains
change+turning) ?	churning
charlatan+parade) ?	charade
chemical+mystery) ?	chemistry
chi+arrange) ?	change
chi+angle) ?	change
chick+burp) ?	chirp
chick+hen) ?	chicken
chick+kin) ?	chicken
chick+peep) ?	cheep
chick+wrens) ?	chickens
Chi+rise+stop) ?	Christ
chirp+peep) ?	cheep
choke+berry) ?	cherry
Christ+i+am) ?	Christian
Christ+mass) ?	Christmas

christmas+**jingle**) ?	Cringle
chrono**logy**+**logical**) ?	chronological
Chronos+the**ology**) ?	chronology
church+**pole**) ?	chapel
circumfrence+**arc**+**all**) ?	circle
circle+**come**+**reference**) ?	circumference
circle**+enter**) ?	center
circle+**stance**) ?	circumstance
circle+**com**mon+**stance**) ?	circumstance
circle+**us**) ?	circus
circumfrence+cur**ling**) ?	circling
city+**dell**) ?	citadel
city+**sons**) ?	citizens
clap+**loud**) ?	applaud
class+**st**ay) ?	caste
clean+**air**) ?	clear
clear+**l**+**find**) ?	clarify
cling+**paw**) ?	claw
cloister**+tro**pic+**phobic**) ?	claustrophobic
corn+you+**copi**ous) ?	cornucopia
close+**asp**) ?	clasp
close+**cues**) ?	clues
closed+**glued**) ?	kluge
close+**snip**) ?	clip
closed+p**ass**) ?	class
close+**pause**) ?	clause
close+**pinch**) ?	clinch
close+**wrench**) ?	clenched
clap+**wack**) ?	clack
close+**slap**) ?	clap
cloth+**those**) ?	clothes
clothes+**it**) ?	closet
change+ad**vance**) ?	chance
chant+**harm**ony) ?	charm
chant+**near**) ?	cheer
chart+**graph**ic+**see**) ?	cartography
chor**ds**+**us**) ?	chorus
Christ+**mass**) ?	Christmas
crystal+**mist**) ?	crystmist/Christmas
clod+**dump**) ?	clump
close+**aim**) ?	claim
close+**pinch**) ?	clinch
close+**wrench**) ?	clench
cloth+**those**) ?	clothes

cluck+hutch) ?	clutch
clump+blot) ?	clot
coal+tar) ?	char
coffee+fiend) ?	caffeine
collect+show+one) ?	collection
collide+clapse) ?	collapse
collide+shown) ?	collision
comes+it) ?	comet
comment+pain) ?	complain
common+pair) ?	compare
common+passion) ?	compassion
common+unity) ?	community
communicate+mental) ?	comment
communicate+passion) ?	compassion
come+apprehend) ?	comprehend
come+pass) ?	compass
come+unity) ?	community
come+mutal+unity) ?	community
comply+illicit) ?	complicit
comply+pleasant) ?	complacent
comply+alliance) ?	compliance
common+parts) ?	compare
come+one) ?	common
comments+mend) ?	commend
common+binding) ?	combining
common+pact) ?	compact
common+incidence) ?	coincidence
common+promising) ?	compromising
common+unity+make) ?	communicate
comment+demand) ?	commands
comment+pain) ?	complain
connect+gregarious+essence) ?	congress
compete+it+shown) ?	competition
compilant+illicit) ?	complicit
concept+shown) ?	conception
connect+gregarious+make) ?	congregate
connect+jump+relate) ?	conjugate
connect+make) ?	kinetic
conscious+affirms) ?	confirms
conscious+descend) ?	condescend
conscious+current) ?	concur
conscious+knit) ?	connect
conscious+knot) ?	connect
conscious+center+make) ?	concentrate

conscious+evidence) ?	confidence
conscious+gratitude+elated+shown	congratulation
conscious+inverts) ?	converts
conscious+kluge) ?	conclude
conscious+occur) ?	concur
consciously+reserve) ?	conserve
conscious+see+i+have) ?	conceive
conscious+travel+roll) ?	control
conscious+seal) ?	conceals
conscious+scientist+of+us) ?	conscientious
conscious+spiral) ?	conspire
conscious+verse+say+shown)?	conversation
constrict+rein) ?	constrain
continue+tag+us) ?	contagious
continue+insist+stand) ?	consistent
continued+rules) ?	controls
continue+stand) ?	constant
controlled+form+did) ?	conformed
control+insist+stance) ?	consistent
control+verse+i+all) ?	controversial
control+victum) ?	convict
control+vindicate) ?	convince
constant+sonic+stance) ?	consonant
conquer+quest) ?	conquest
conscious+star+tell+make+shown)?	constellations
coughing+in) ?	coffin
combined+order+made+did) ?	coordinated
comment+demand) ?	command
commerce+show+all) ?	commercials
common+panel+see) ?	company
communicate+posed) ?	composed
comply+penned+be) ?	company
community+merchandise) ?	commerce
comrade+are+we) ?	comradery
concentrate+tense+shown) ?	contention
cone+center+make) ?	concentrate
congregate+elate+shown) ?	congratulation
comply+penned+satiate)?	compensate
concentrate+tense+shown) ?	contension
conclude+profess) ?	confess
cone+retains) ?	contains
confess+hide) ?	confide
connect+influences) ?	confluences
conscious+deemed) ?	condemned

Conscious+fuse+us) ?	Confucius
conscious+secret+make) ?	consecrated
consistant+seal) ?	conceal
constant+sonic+stance) ?	consonance
continue+stand+it) ?	constant
conscious+damn) ?	condemn
conscious+fidelity) ?	confide
conscious+stellar+shown) ?	constellation
conscious+dammed) ?	condemned
control+insist+stance) ?	consistant
controled+tenet) ?	content
connect+center+make) ?	concentrate
control+adversarial) ?	controversial
controversial+dictions) ?	contradictions
cooked+eats) ?	cookies
correct+relation) ?	correlations
correct+responding) ?	corresponding
correct+story) ?	rectory
correlated+right) ?	correct
core+operate+shown) ?	corporation
corona+net) ?	coronet
coronet+round) ?	crown
couple+inclusion) ?	collusion
curve+over) ?	cover
cool+old) ?	cold
coughing+in) ?	coffin
coven+act) ?	covenant
convene+shown) ?	convention
cover+get) ?	covet
covered+dirt) ?	covert
cover+inverted) ?	covert
covert+hidden) ?	coven
cower+hunch) ?	crouch
cow+herds) ?	cowards
crack+bunching) ?	crunching
crack+dust) ?	crust
cracker+munchy) ?	crunchy
crashing+rests) ?	crests
crack+rumble) ?	crumble
crash+rush) ?	crush
crate+handle) ?	cradle
crawl+sneak) ?	creep
crease+abyss) ?	crevice
crack+vast) ?	crevice

crate+raft) ?	craft
crime+animal) ?	criminal
cringe+wrinkle) ?	crinkle
cringe+tingle) ?	Cringle
critic+eyes) ?	criticize
crud+rude) ?	crude
cringe+wrinkle) ?	crinkle
crux+stop+mast) ?	Xmas
cry+is) ?	crisis
crying+isis) ?	crisis
cry+me) ?	crime
crystal+round) ?	crown
cross+X) ?	crux
crucify+fixture) ?	crucifix
crucify+parades) ?	crusades
crud+rude) ?	crude
cry+stop) ?	Christ
curve+swirling) ?	curling
curve+up) ?	cup
cusses+verse) ?	curses
cut+ill) ?	kill
cyclic+of+logic) ?	"cyclology"
cycle+logic+all) ?	psychologica
D) ?down	**Down**
dammed+aged) ?	damaged
dammed+bastard+be) ?	dastardly
date+tally) ?	data
day+at+make) ?	date
day+dream) ?	daydream
delicious+lights) ?	delights
diarrhea+wiper) ?	diaper
dictate+shown) ?	dictations
die+eat) ?	diet
die+fire) ?	dire
dim+minimize+finish) ?	diminish
dire+rightly) ?	directly
dire+right+shown) ?	direction
dirt+gust) ?	dust
disappointed+gust) ?	disgust
disciple+line) ?	discipline
discovered+cipher) ?	deciphered
dissed+turbulent) ?	disturbed
distribute+place) ?	display
divide+force) ?	divorce

divide+refer) ?	differ
divided+angle) ?	diagonal
divided+ein/one) ?	divine
divide+veer+edge) ?	diverge
dip+hole) ?	dimple
djin+is) ?	genius
discuss+scribe) ?	describe
diss+cuss) ?	disgust
dis+crime+i+make+shown) ?	discrimination
dis+speak+able) ?	despicable
dismal+function) ?	malfunction
divide+ill) ?	devil
dead+desserted) ?	desert
deal+tells) ?	details
dead+theos) ?	death
deceive+concept+shown) ?	deception
decide+inferring) ?	deciphering
décor+made+did) ?	decorated
deep+neigh) ?	deny
deep+pressing) ?	depressing
deep+leery+us) ?	delirious
deep+theos) ?	depth
define+it+shown) ?	definition
defy+not+be) ?	defiantly
delicate+see) ?	delicacy
delightful+dish+us) ?	delicious
delicacy+dish+us) ?	delicious
delicacy+lick+is) ?	delicious
deli+light+full) ?	delightful
demagogue+god) ?	demigod
demon+crazy) ?	democracy
demon+money+seek) ?	demonic
demons+comanding) ?	demanding
descent+round) ?	Down
describe+inscriptions) ?	descriptions
deserve+it) ?	dessert
design+make) ?	designate
destruct+noise+did) ?	destroyed
despair+make) ?	desparate
determined+fine) ?	defined
destroy+integrate) ?	disintegrate
detain+attention) ?	detention
determines+sides) ?	decides
devil+is) ?	devious

devolved+illusion) ?	delusion
devout+be) ?	devotee
devout+emotion) ?	devotion
diagonal+cabol+it+all) ?	diabolical
different+mental+shown) ?	dimensions
dim+minimize+show+did) ?	diminished
divided+angle) ?	diagonal
divide+ends) ?	dividends
divide+force) ?	divorce
divide+vision) ?	division
divine+made+shown) ?	divination
divine+out) ?	devout
doll+other) ?	daughter
donor+make) ?	donate
dote+repeat) ?	Daughter
double+be+is) ?	dubious
down+anger)	danger
down+arc) ?	dark
down+asterisk) ?	disaster
down+bump) ?	dump
down+earth) ?	death
down+meaning) ?	demeaning
down+well) ?	dwell
down+pimple) ?	dimple
down+a+star) ?	disaster
down+evil) ?	devil
down+evening+ill) ?	devil
down+feeted) ?	defeated
down+luge) ?	deluge
down+murmur) ?	demur
down+pronounce) ?	denounce
down+rain) ?	drain
down+recline) ?	declines
down+sun) ?	done
downy+dunk) ?	ducks
dragon+i+am) ?	draconian
drag+on) ?	dragon
drag+rift) ?	drift
drain+down) ?	drown
drain+plop) ?	drop
dramatic+harmony+karma) ?	dharma
draw+drop+make) ?	drapes
dream+dead) ?	dread
drip+plop) ?	drop

dribble+**drool**	drivel
drop+**fizzles**) ?	drizzles
drop+**shift**) ?	drift
drown+**hazy**) ?	drowsy
drown+**hug**) ?	drug
drop+shift) ?	drift
dry+**out**) ?	drought
drug+**drin**k) ?	drunk
drug+**fun**k) ?	drunk
dumb+**men**tal+**sho**wn+**have**) ?	dementia
duel+**reality**) ?	duality
dubious+**compli**city) ?	duplicity
duplex+**soli**citous) ?	duplicitous
duplicitous+**tr**ouble) ?	double
dust+**shov**eled) ?	dishevel
dust+**sk**y) ?	dusk
dust+eternity) ?	destiny
E) ?	**East, Even, Energy**
early+**the**ta) ?	earth
East+**gull**) ?	eagle
east+**star**) ?	Easter
eat+**able**) ?	edible
ecstatic+**fant**asy) ?	ecstasy
Egypt+**see**) ?	gypsie
electric+**cut**) ?	electrocute
elevate+**high**+**home**) ?	Elohiem
elusive+**in**+**i**+**am**) ?	Eleusinian
element+**ange**ls) ?	elementals
elevate+**make**) ?	elate
elevate+**men**tal+**are**+**thee**) ?	elementary
emo+**evok**e) ?	emote
emote+**shown**) ?	emotion
emperor+**pyr**amid) ?	empire
en**chan**ted+**harm**ony+**doing**) ?	charming
en**chan**ting+**shown**) ?	incantations
end+**of**+**me**) ?	enemy
end+**sure**) ?	endure
energy+**con**+**of**+**me**) ?	economy
energy+**lift**+**make**) ?	elevate
energy+**motion**) ?	emotion
energy+**quali**ty) ?	equal
energy+**stir**+**gen**eration) ?	Estrogen
energy+**vacu**um+**make**) ?	evacuate
energy+**vapor**+**make**) ?	evaporate

energy+**motion**) ?	emotion
enter+**fear**) ?	Interfere
enter+**obtain**) ?	entertain
ent**ertaining**+**nice**) ?	enticing
equal+**night/not/nox**) ?	equinox
erect+**make**) ?	erotic
ero**s**+**rouse**) ?	arouse
ess**ence**+**all**+**be**) ?	essentially
ess**ence**+**it**+**all**) ? learn**ester**+**scent**+**all**]**E**ssential	essential
ess**ence**+**make**) ?	estimate
ess**ential**+**s**ence) ?	essence
e**strogen**+**repeat**) ?	Easter
e**vening**+**ill**) ?	evil
eye+**doll**) ?	idol
extra+**central**+**magic**) ?	eccentric
extra+**crucial**+**making**) ?	excruciating
exist+**essential**) ?	existential
exit+**cluged**) ?	excluded
extra+**inciting**) ?	exciting
extra+**plain**) ?	explain
extra+**speak**+**plain**) ?	explain
extra+**speed**+**it**) ?	expedite
extra+**spend**+**i**+**have**) ?	expensive
F) ?	**Future, Flow**
fab+**brick**+**made**) ?	fabricated
fable+**nebu**lous) ?	fabulous
fact+**actual**) ?	factual
fact+**make**) ?	fake
fall+**ail**) ?	fail
fail+**all**) ?	fall
fair+**airy**) ?	fairy
fall+**low**) ?	follow
fall+**see**+**be**) ?	falsely
fall+**sh**a**de**) ?	fade
fall+**somers**a**ult**) ?	fault
fall+**tumble**) ?	fumble
false+**diction**) ?	fiction
famil**iar**+**of**+**us**) ?	famous
family+**you**+**are**) ?	familiar
fam**ine**+**vani**shed) ?	famished
fam**ous**+**name**) ?	fame
fan+**est**a**tic**) ?	fanatic
fan+**lun**a**tic**) ?	fanatic

fantasy+pl**astic**) ?	fantastic
fans+**see**) ?	fancy
far+d**ate**/g**ate**) ?	fate
fare+**fee**) ?	free
farm+and+**seed**s) ?	pharmacy
fastened+**make**) ?	fascinate
fasten+**see**+m**aking**) ?	fascinating
fate+**the**os) ?	faith
fatal+**it**+be) ?	atality
fate+**all**) ?	fatal
fate+truth) ?	faith
favor+**right**) ?	favorite
feast+**i**+have) ?	festive
feed+**eat**+**stop**) ?	feast
feed+g**ood**) ?	food
feed+**stay**) ?	fiesta
fell+**lonely**) ?	felony
fell+**one**) ?	felon
feral+**raucous**) ?	ferocious
festive+**all**) ?	festival
ficticious+**shown**) ?	fiction
fighting+**stay**) ?	feisty
filling+**yield**) ?	fields
fill+**hole**) ?	full
final+see) ?	finale
find+gr**ound**) ?	found
find+d**own**) ?	found
fine+**right**) ?	ripe
finish+**all**) ?	final
finish+**all**) ?	fall
finish+**fast**) ?	first
fin+is+**shown**) ?	finish
fin+**near**) ?	fear
fire+**lick**+**re**peat) ?	flicker
fired+**ored**) ?	forged
fire+pi**erce**) ?	fierce
flame+w**ick**+repeat) ?	flicker
flab+fatt**y**) ?	flabby
flab+**gasp**) ?	flabbergast
flaccid+**ab**domen) ?	flab
flash+**shown**) ?	fashion
flat+story) ?	flattery
flexing+**lux**) ?	flux
flower+s**avor**+ful**l**) ?	flavorful

126

flower+nou**rishing**) ?	flourishing
flow+fast+**sh**own) ?	lash
flow+**high**) ?	fly
flow+g**littering**) ?	flittering
flow+**lutes**) ?	flutes
flow+**sky**+**wing**) ?	flying
flow+sl**oppy**) ?	floppy
fluttering+**by**) ?	butterflies
fly+he**ight**) ?	flight
flying+**owl**) ?	fowl
fly+**air**+be) ?	fairy
fly+**rag**) ?	flag
fly+t**ow**) ?	flow
foes+fi**ght**) ?	fought
force+**right**) ?	fight
follow+**lock**) ?	flock
food+**eat**+did) ?	feed
food+**need**) ?	feed
for**get**+**give**) ?	forgive
former+**come**) ?	from
form+**made**+**sh**own) ?	formation
for+**rest**) ?	forest
forest+gor**aged**) ?	forage
fort+at**titude**) ?	fortitude
fortune+**make**) ?	fortunate
force+to**ward**) ?	forward
forward+b**all**) ?	fall
forward+**warned**) ?	forewarned
found+**act**) ?	fact
frac**tal**+**sh**own) ?	fraction
fracture+**crack**) ?	frack
fractured+**factual**) ?	fractal
fractured+**rag**+rem**nants**) ?	fragments
fragile+fa**il**) ?	frail
frequent+s**equence**) ?	frequencies
friend+b**ond**+be) ?	fondly
fright+**near**) ?	fear
fright+regr**et**) **?**	fret
fro+**come**) ?	from
from+**where**) ?	former
found+**actual**) ?	fact
frozen+**mist**) ?	frost
fuck+**you**+**show**+**ma**) ?	Fukushima
fuel+sp**ire**) ?	fire

full+**at**+**be**) ?	fatty
fury+**is**+**us**) ?	furious
future+all) ?	fall
future+**date**) ?	fate
future+virility) ?	fertility
G) ?	**God, Good, Glitter, Great**
gag+**sp**eak) ?	gasp
gang+mon**ster**) ?	gangsters
gassy+**g**ust+be) ?	ghastly
gave+**lift**) ?	gift
gene+**be**) ?	genie
gene+era+make+shown) ?	generations
gene+gno**sis**) ?	genesis
genes+of+**Isis**) ?	genesis
genes+**rate**+**shown**) ?	generation
genie/dj**in**)+he**X**) ?	jinx
gent+sub**tle**) ?	gentle
gent+vile) ?	gentile
geode+**ology**) ?	geology
geology+g**raph**+see) ?	geography
ghost+**soul**) ?	ghoul
ghost+**spells**) ?	gospels
give+h**ave**) ?	gave
give+**lift**) ?	gift
glasses+g**aze**) ?	glaze
glee+h**ad**) ?	glad
globe+ball) ?	global
glory+**f**ind) ?	glorify
glow+**amorous**) ?	glamorous
glow+**be**) ?	glee
glow+d**oom**) ?	gloom
glow+**litter**) ?	glitter
glow+**over**+**be**) ?	globe
glow+**ray**) ?	glory
glow+spl**endid**) ?	Glenda
glow+st**are**) ?	glare
glow+st**ory**) ?	glory
glow+stream) ?	gleam
glue+**in**) ?	gluten
gluten+chewy) ?	gooey
glut+**in**) ? **gut**+**on**) ?	glutton
God – **G**) ?	odd
God+**host**) ?	ghost
Gods+**fate**) ?	gate

God+**spell**) ?	gospel
go+lull+be) ?	gully
Good+**awed** ?	God
go+out) ?	gut
Go+over+mental) ?	governmental
go+at) **?**	get
go+to) ?	got
gouge+ru**dder**) ?	gutter
grab+**asp**) ?	grasp
grab+**clasp**) ?	grasp
grab+**need**) ?	greed
grace+full+see) ?	gracefully
grace+show+us) ?	gracious
grade+you+make) ?	graduate
grade+you+make+**shown**) ?	graduation
grain+**fine**) ?	grind
grand+mother) ?	Grandma
grateful+**attitude**) ?	gratitude
grave+**vital**+is) ?	gravitas
great+**full**) ?	grateful
great+n**eed**) ?	greed
greed+**nab**) ?	grab
green+**go**) ?	grow
green+**low**) ?	grow
green+**sow**) ?	grow
grid+**gate**) ?	grate
grind+**down**) ?	ground
greed+**shift**) ?	grift
greed+**shaft**) ?	graft
grip+**nab**) ?	grab
grow+**circle**+see) ?	grocery
grow+d**own**) ?	ground
groan+**howl**) ?	growl
groove+**cove**) ?	grove
grow+d**own**)	ground
growl+d**ump**) ?	grump
growl+**gut**) ?	grunt
growl+m**oan**) ?	groan
growl+mu**mble**) ?	grumble
growl+**rough**) ?	gruff
gu**ess**+make) ?	estimate
gu**st**+host) ?	ghost
gut+**est**imate) ?	guess
H) ?	**Heal, Half, Hold**

hallowed+bet**ween**) ?	Halloween
halo+ho**llow**) ?	hallowed
hand+h**old**) ?	handle
happens+**hazzardly**) ?	haphazardly
happy+**open**) ?	hope
happy+op**ening**) ?	happening
happy+**stance**) ?	happenstance
happy+tri**ppy**) ?	hippy
harmony+fe**ast**) ?	harvest
hat+**bit**) ?	habit
haven+**even**) ?	heaven
have+**old**) ?	hold
head+**ears**) ?	hear
heal+**even**) ?	heaven
heal+**thee**) ?	health
hear+**did**) ?	heard
hear+**lead**) ?	heed
heart+earth) ?	hearth
heat+**earth**) ?	hearth
heave+very	heavy
heed+**ear**) ?	hear
help+**ill**) ?	heal
heredity+empr**ess**) ?	heiress
her+**him**+**me**+**is**) ?	Hermes
herm+**Aphrodite**) ?	hermaphrodite
hide+b**unker**) ?	hunker
hide+**burrow**+**makes**) ? hide+bear+make	hibernates
hide+**to**+**us**) ?	hideous
high+**arch**+**key**) ?	hierarchy
high+b**ump**) ?	hump
high+**cock**) ?	hawk
high+**curling**) ?	hurling
high+**happy**) ?	hippie
high+**sight**) ?	height
high+**per**son) ?	hyper
high+**pose**+**thesis**) ?	hypothesis
hip+gypsie) ?	hippie
hippie+knot+**eyes**+did) ?	hypnotized
his+**store**+be) ?	history
his+**story**) ?	history
hold+**arm**+**my**+**needs**) ?	harmony
hold+**even**) ?	heaven
hold+m**eld**) ?	held
hold+**open**) ?	hope

hole+toe) ?	hoe
hole+wore) ?	whore
holy+day) ?	holiday
Holy+is+magic) ?	holistic
holy+Om) ?	home
holy+order) ?	hour
honorable+best) ?	honest
hood+bum) ?	hoodlum
hood+slum) ?	hoodlum
hoof+groove)	hoove
hoot+growl) ?	howl
horror+terrific) ?	horrific
Horus+rise+on) ?	horizon
horror+make+all+be)	horrifically
Horus+risen) ?	horizon
Horus+telescope) ?	horoscope
host+vile) ?	hostile
human+i+be) ?	humanity
humid+moss) ?	humus
humus+man) ?	human
humble+fragility) ?	humility
humble+little+made) ?	humiliate
hump+pyramid) ?	umpire
Hun+agrarian) ? hunker+agriculture+aryan	Hungarian
hunker+cuddle) ?	huddle
hurt+arm) ?	harm
hyper+of+critic) ?	hypocrite
hypnotic+eyes) ?	hypnotize
hypnotize+crazy) ?	hypocrisy
hypnotize+gnosis) ?	hypnosis
I) ?	Inner
id+doll) ?	idol
idea+ot) ?	idiot
idea+real) ?	ideal
Ide+enter+thee) ?	identity
Ide+real) ?	ideal
ides+At) ?	idea
Ides+ology) ?	ideology
id+is+ot) ?	idiot
idol+a+treasure) ?	idolatry
ill+literature+made) ?	illiterate
Ill+ledger+able) ?	illegible
illuminate+to+us) ?	luminous

illumination+not+see) ?	illuminati
illusive+shown) ?	illusion
image+i+make+shown) ?	imagination
impress+shown) ?	impression
in+augment+intergrate) ?	inaugurate
in+center) ?	enter
in+chant+sing) ?	enchanting
in+closed+shown) ?	inclusion
increase+clime) ?	incline
in+decent) ?	indecent
in+depend+dance) ?	independence
Indian+genesis) ?	indigenous
ingenious+seer) ?	engineer
in+joy) ?	enjoy
in+near) ?	inner
inner+attain+mental) ?	entertainment
inner+cents+i+have) ?	incentive
Inner+fasen+you+make) ?	infatuate
inner+fill+make) ?	inflate
inner+formation) ?	information
inner+genie+you+be) ?	ingenuity
inner+genius) ?	ingenious
inner+hailing) ?	inhaling
inner+lighting) ?	enlighting
inner+no+sense) ?	innocence
inner+say+fault) ?	insult
inner+sides) ?	insides
inner+sight) ?	Insight
inner+still) ?	instill
inner+sex+shown) ?	intersection
inner+structure+shown) ?	instruction
inner+tense) ?	intense
inner+obtain+mental) ?	entertainment
inner+magic+make+shown) ?	imagination
inner+net) ?	internet
inner+trigger) ?	intrigue
inner+view) ?	interview
inner+spiral+shown) ?	inspiration
I+no) ?	in
in+not+delete+able) ?	indelible
I+not+dividable+all) ?	individual
in+scents) ?	incense
in+side+of+us) ?	insidious
in+strum+acts) ?	instruments

intel+allegence) ?	intelligence
instruments+mental) ?	instrumentals
intelligence+connect+you+all) ?	intellectual
in+tell) ?	intel
in+tie+angle) ?	intangle
in+timid+make) ?	intimidate
into+rude) ?	intrude
in+toxic+make+did) ?	intoxicated
Invent+nova+make)?	inovate
is+sense) ?	essence
is+spy+knowledge) ?	espionage
it+is) ?	tis
it+was) ?	twas
I+would+have) ?	I'da
J) ?	**Judge, Joke, Jump**
Jack+up) ?	jump
jar+mug) ?	jug
jab+in) ?	javelins
job+ligature+engage) ?	obligate
join+function) ?	junction
jolly+tingle) ?	jingle
jolt+up) ?	jump
Judge+at+ill) ?	Jail
Judge+essence+us ?	Jesus
judge+hear) ?	jeer
jump+obligation) ?	job
jump+volt) ?	jolt
jumpy+flunkie) ?	junkie
junk+tangle) ?	jungle
jungle+bramble) ?	jumble
just+i+find ?	justify
K) ?	**Connect, Quest, Choice**
kin+ring) ?	king
king+dome ?	kingdom
knee+angle) ?	kneel
knit+thought) ?	knot
knob+hole) ?	knoll
knot+show) ?	know
know+all) ?	Noah
know+alleged) ?	knowledge
know+name+on) ?	gnomon
know+right) ?	knights
known+able) ?	noble
known+slave) ?	knaves

L) ?	Light, Lack
lang**u**age+**myth**+mathemat**ics**)?	langmythics
lay+ea**sy**) ?	lazy
lay+**fall**) ?	lull
lay+**sure**) ?	leisure
lead+**edge**) ?	ledge
le**a**ve+aft) ?	left
le**a**ve+get) ?	let
leg**a**l+**it**+make) ?	legitimate
leg**a**l+**state**+d**oers**) ?	legislators
leg**a**ra+**all**) ?	legal
leg+c**apture**) ?	ligature
len**d**+let) ?	lent
lie+**in**) ?	liom
like+**com**ment+subs**cribe**	likecomscribe
le**tter**+**really**) ?	literally
le**tter**+**rate**+s**ure**) ?	literature
lewd+**hear**) ?	leer
lead+**edge**) ?	ledge
len**d**+let) ?	lent
ling**u**istic+**usage**) ?	language
link+**guess**+my**stic**) ?	linguistic
link+**quest**+make+**see**) ?	linguistically
lip+**sp**it) ?	lisp
lip+ga**sp**) ?	lisp
liter**a**ry+fea**ture**) ?	literature
Livable – **Li**) ?	viable
log**o**s+make) ?	logic
lon**g**+**t**o+**h**old) ?	leng**th**
longing+**h**ang+you+**sh**own) **?**	languish
long+**st**op) ?	lost
lo**n**ging+**only**) ?	lonely
look+**earn**) ?	learn
low+c**rude**) ?	lewd
low+**d**own) ?	load
low+**lift**) ?	loft
low+**fall**) ?	lull
low+**only**) **?** low+**one**+**be**) ?	lonely
low+**the**ta+did) ?	loathed
lude+grote**sque**) ?	ludicrous
M) ?	Mind, Magi, Man, Myth, Mother
make+**son**) ?	mason
make+**use**) ?	muse
ma**k**e+**right**) ?	might

malaise+vicious) ?	malicious
mammary+animal)?	mammal
magi+calculate) ?	magical
magi+connect+make) ?	magnetic
magic+doll+seen) ?	Magdalene
man+dominate) ?	mandates
magic+I+am) ?	magician
magi+make) ?	magic
magi+trick) ?	magic
man+be) ?	manly
manage+mental) ?	management
man+cage) ?	manage
man+dictate) ?	mandate
man+i+political+made+shown) ?	manipulation
manual+script) ?	manuscripts
many+men) ?	man
mare+carriage) ? marry+age) ?	marriage
mark+get) ?	market
mark+X) ?	marks
mash+low) ?	mow
masked+parade) ?	masquerade
mass+acres) ?	massacres
master+son) ?	masons
mast+steer) ?	master
mast+steer+make+shown) ?	masterbation
math+magical) ?	mathematical
math+material+i+show+i+am) ?	mathematician
maternity+harmony) ?	matrimony
matt+rest) ?	mattress
mean+ass) ?	menace
mean+had) ?	mad
medicine+make) ?	medicate
medium+fiddle) ?	meddle
medium+see+in) ?	medicine
me+essence+say+did) ?	messaged
me+eye) ?	my
me+I) ?	my
me+id+stop) ?	midst
mellow+and+holy) ?	melancholy
mellow+dramatic) ?	melodramatic
meld+smelt) ?	melt
melt+low) ?	mellow
mend+weld) ?	meld
men+seize) ?	menses

men+stance) ?	menace
men+**straight**) ?	menstruate
men+**pause**) ?	menopause
mental+**shown**) ?	mention
mental+tut**or**) ?	mentor
merchant+para**dise**) ?	merchandise
meter+g**nom**on) ?	metronome
meter+**name**) ?	metronome
meter+**sure**+d**id**) ?	measured
mid+**day**) ?	median
mid+**diem**) ?	medium
middle+one/i**ne**) ?	mine
mid+**hole**) ?	middle
mid+**inner**+**l**de) ?	mind
mid+**st**op) ?	midst
mildew+**old**) ?	mold
mind+l+**stir**) ?	minister
mind+l+**store**) ?	minister
mind+**moved**) ?	mood
mini+**min**u**te**) ?	minutes
miracle+ne**bul**ous) ?	miraculous
mirror+im**ages**) ?	mirages
mirror+**talk**) ?	mock
mirth+**airy**) ?	merry
mischief+**evil**+**is**) ?	mischievous
miser+**able**) ?	miserable
miss+**constru**cted+g**lued**) ?	misconstrued
miss+**take**n) ?	mistake
mistake+**spellings**) ?	misspellings
mist+**story**) ?	mystery
mist+**theos**) ?	myth
mob+mon**ster**) ?	mobster
modern+**doll**) ?	model
mold+**dew**) ?	mildew
mold+d**usty**) ?	musty
Moon+**day**) ?	Monday
moon+**ocean**) ?	motion
moon+**stir**) ?	monster
moon+**theos**+**see**) ?	monthly
moon+**theta**) ?	month
mortality+en**gage**) ?	mortgage
mouse+**h**oles) ?	moles
move+**did**) ?	mood
move+**ocean**) ?	motion

mud+**puddle**) ?	muddle
music+i+**am**) ?	musician
my+**aid** = ?	maid
my+end) ?	mind
my+**id**) ?	mid
my+**in**) ?	mine
my+**nee**d) ?	money
my+**other**) ?	mother
my+**right**) ?	might
mystery+mag**ic**) ?	mystic
mythic+**all**) ?	mythical
mythical+**story**) ?	mystery
myth+mag**ic**) ?	mythic
N) ?	**No, Negative, Nature**
natal+ac**tivity**) ?	nativity
native+**shown**) ?	nation
nature+**all**) ?	natural
natural+**live**) ?	native
nature+**real**) ?	natural
navy+**aviate**) ?	navigate
neck+**lace**) ?	necklace
negative+**go**+l+m**ake**+**showns**) ?	negotiations
net+**st**ick) ?	nest
new+**over**+**ab**ove) ?	nova
nip+hole) ?	nipple
no+at) ?	not
no+engage**+make**) ?	negate
no+**light**) ?	night
none+**sense**) ?	nonsense
norm+**all**) ?	normal
no+**one**) ?	none
no+go+make+l+have) ?	negative
not+**either**) ?	neither
not+**ever**) ?	never
note+i+**see**) ?	notice
note+**right**+be) ?	notoriety
not+**ever**) ?	never
not+**evil**) ?	naïve
not+fair+be+us) ?	nefarious
no+repeat+**th**eta) ?	north
noted+**right**+th**ee**) ?	notoriety
not+**same**) ?	insane
not+**tasty**) ?	nasty
no+**thing**) ?	nothing

not+victim+able) ?	invincible
nourishes+surely) ?	nurtures
now+ear) ?	near
now+feed) ?	need
now+views) ?	news
nox/night+toxic) ?	noxious
nutrient+shown) ?	nutrition
nut+tree+delicious) ?	nutritious
O) ?	**Oll/All, Round, Mouth**
obedient+ligature+engaged) ?	obligate
object+i+have) ?	objective
objective+essence) ?	obsess
object+stack+hole) ?	obstacle
object+structure) ?	obstruct
obscur+scene) ?	obscene
occasion+current) ?	occur
off+fence+end) ?	offend
old+in) ?	Odin
om+mega) ?	omega
one+be) ?	only
open+port+unity) ?	opportunity
oppose+it) ?	opposite
optical+mystic) ?	optimistic
options+mystery+seek) ?	optimistic
oral+make+did) ?	orated
orbit+torus) ?	oraborus
ore+of+mint) ?	ornament
origin+all) ?	original
Orion+Sirius) ?	Osiris
oround+it) ?	orbit
oround+us) ?	Ouranus
out+there) ?	outer
out+theres) ?	others
out+they+are+is) ?	others
over+above+torus) ?	oraborus
P) ?	**Power, Plant, Pi**
pack+it) ?	pocket
pair+like+rail) ?	parallel
participate+raid) ?	parade
party+raid) ?	parade
pass+shown) ?	passion
pass+stop) ?	past
pass+quest) ?	pasque
pasque+al) ?	Pasqual

past+store) ?	pastor
paternal+riot) ?	patriot
paternal+roll) ?	patrol
path+way/pass+age) ?	passage
pay+gain) ?	pain
peer+concept+shown) ?	perception
peer+see+i+have) ?	perceive
pentagram+tentacle) ?	pentacle
people+nation) ?	population
per+fact) ?	perfect
perfect+form+dance) ?	performance
persevere+insist) ?	persistent
pervert+verse) ?	perverse
pestilence+mystery+see) ?	pessimistic
pet+testy) ?	pesty
pew+soup) ?	poop
phantom+see) ?	fantasy
photon+graphic) ?	Photograph /faux
physical+I+am) ?	physician
pig+ugly) ?	pug
place+at) ?	plant
place+cause) ?	plause
place+lot) ?	plot
plant+network) ?	planet
plat+tableau) ?	plateaus
play+space) ?	place
plause+able) ?	possible
play+sure) ?	pleasure
plea+alege) ?	pledge
plea+ease) ?	please
plea+lead) ?	plead
plea+need ?	plead
please+many) ?	plenty
pleasing+essence) ?	pleasant
please+sure) ?	pleasure
pliable+mastic) ?	plastic
plot+spaces) ?	places
plow+under) ?	plunder
plump+kinds) ?	pumpkins
plums+pump)	plump
Poe+rhyme) ?	poems
pointy+dimple) ?	pimple
pole+pit) ?	pulpit
pole+nice) ?	police

pomp+circu**s**) ?	pompous
poor-invert+**thee**) ?	poverty
pop+seed**s**) ?	poppies
pop+you+**are**) ?	popular
portable+**trait**) ?	portrait
port+**hole**) ?	portal
portrait+**all**) ?	portrayals
portrait+conve**yed**) ?	portrayed
pose+**sit**+**shown**) ?	position
pot+emo**tion**) ?	potion
potent+eventu**ally**) ?	potentially
potential+**intent**) ?	potent
potent+**shown**) ?	potion
power+**mid**) ?	pyramid
praise+gra**cious**) ?	precious
praise+**say**) ?	pray
praise+**swear**) ?	prayer
pray+**raise**) ?	praise
pray+**rays** ?	praise
pray+**reach**) ?	preach
preceed+re**cession**) ?	precession
precious+re**serve**) ?	preserve
present+make+**shown**) ?	presentation
pressed+**air**) ?	pressure
pretty+d**ance**) ?	prance
prevention+**script**+**shown**) ?	prescription
previous+con**clude**) ?	preclude
previous+**dict**ated+**shown**) ?	prediction
previous+in**tend**) ?	pretend
previous+**decease**+**doer**) ?	predecessor
previously+**pare**) ?	prepare -cut ahead
previous+**tense**) ?	pretenses
prey+**owl**) ?	prowl
priest+**ess**ence) ?	priestess
probe+**able**) ?	probable
probable+**cause**+**able**) ?	plausible
problems+**feign**) ?	profane
proceed+en**dure**) ?	procedure
proceed+**to**+agon**y**+**is**) ?	protagonist
proclaim+**loud**) ?	proud
proclaim+**noun**+**s**ay) ?	pronounce
procreated+**gen**eration+th**ee**) ?	progeny
professional+**jump**+**shown**) ?	projection
profess+**it**) ?	prophet

profess+**repeater**) ?	professor
profuse+**shown**) ?	profusion
project+**rude**) ?	protrude
prophet+po**etic**) ?	prophetic
prophet+**sees**) ?	prophesies
propose+**fate**) ?	prophet
prose+an**nounce**) ?	pronounce
prose+**claim**) ?	proclaim
prose+**holy**+hypno**tize**) ?	proselytize
prosody+**odes**) ?	prose
prostrating+in**stitution**) ?	prostitution
proud+d**ance**) ?	prance
proud+**rude**) ?	prude
proved+**found**) ?	profound
prove+**of**) ?	proofs
provide+**cure**) ?	procure
prune+**rude**) ?	prude
psyche+**delic**acies) ?	psychedelic
public+**show**+do**ing**) ?	publishing
pure+**fact**) ?	perfect
purge+**story**) ?	purgatory
purpose+**pose**) ?	propose
purr+**fume**) ?	perfume
purse+**chase**) ?	purchase
push+**lunge**) ?	plunge
push+**open**) ?	pop
push+**up**) ?	pump
puss+d**imple**) ?	pimple nip bit tip
put+**ark**) ?	parks
put+**end** ?	pen
pyre+**it**) ?	pirate
pyramid+**fire**) ?	pyre
Q) ?	**Question Choice**
quality+**find**) ?	qualified
quantify+**be**) ?	quantity
query+**essence**) ?	quest
quest+**on**) ?	question
question+**drag**+**mire**) ?	quagmire
question+**forum**) ?	quorum
question+**hearing**) ?	queries
question+**is**) ?	quiz
question+**veer**) ?	queer
question+**war**+tan**gle**)	quarrel
quest+**sh**own) ?	question

quick+ups) ? kick+ups) ? **quick+coughs**	hiccups
quip+clack)	quack
R) ?	**Round, Repeating**
rage+ape) ?	rape
Ra+in+bow) ?	rainbow
Ra+Jah) ?	Raja
Rajas+**land**) ?	Rajasthan
rake+**keep**) ?	reap
ramification+**parts**) ?	ramparts
ram+rage) ?	rampage
rape+capture) ?	rapture
rare+thaw) ?	raw
rave+chant) ?	rant
raven+us) ?	ravenous
raving+sav**age**) ?	ravage
Ra+in+bow] ?	rainbow
ray+**bow**) ?	rainbow
ray+**dia**mond+**make**) ?	radiate
ray+dial+far) ?	radar
radiating+d**azzle**	razzle
ready+up) ?	red up
real+all+it+be) ?	reality
real+see+it) ?	receipt
real+tired) ? **repeat+tired**) ?	retired
reap+ape) ?	rape
reap+take) ?	rake
reap+c**apture**) ?	rapture
rear+**verse**s) ?	reverse
recall+**collection**) ?	recollection
re**cline+lax**) ?	relax
red+d**ust**) ?	rust
refer+see) ?	referee
re**gal+gala**) ?	regalia
re**gal+lig**ature+**shown**) ?	religion
regime+mind) ?	regiment
regular+make)	regulate
re**lax**+add**itive**) ?	laxative
re**new+vital+live**) ?	revive
repeat+evolve) ?	revolve
re**peat+flakes+sp**ec+**shown**) ?	reflection
re**peat+generating**) ?	regenerating
re**peat+habit+build+make**) ?	rehabilitate
re**peat+i+see**) ?	rise
re**peat+lig**ature+**make**) ?	relegate

repeat+ligature**+on**) ?	religion
repeat+low) ?	row
repeat+new+make+it) ?	renovate
repeat+solve) ?	resolve
repeat+sonorant+ma**ke**) ?	resonate
repeat+Surya**+erect**) ?	resurrect
repress+sent+i**+have**) ?	representatives
republic+i**+am**) ?	Republican
re**pulsive+pug+act**) ?	repugnant
respond**+sensibly**) ?	responsibly
restore+act) ?	restaurant
rest+store) ?	restore
re**peat+solve**) ?	resolve
repeat+tally+make) ?	retaliate
reveal**+rela**te**+shown**) ?	revelation
re+veiling) ?	revealing
revel+bulls) ?	rebels
revolt**+solution**) ?	revolution
revolve+mind+essen**ce**) ?	reminisce
revving**+liven+ring**) ?	reviving
rhythm**+time**) ?	rhymes
right+be**+us**) ?	righteous
right**+story**) ?	rectory
rites+you+all) ?	rituals
rob+in+hood) ?	Robinhood
rolling+t**oast**) ?	roast
roll+tumble) ?	rumble
rose+crux+i**+am**) ?	Rosicrucian
rotor+make) ?	rotate
round+singing) ?	ringing
route**+in**) ?	routine
rubble+publish) ?	rubbish
rut+repeat) ?	rudder
S) ?	**See, Show, Sign, Plural**
sacks+walk ?	socks
sacred+crucified+see) ?	sacrifice
sacred+mental) ?	sacrament
sacred+of+sanctuary)	sacrosanct
sacrifice+red) ?	sacred
saint+Above) ?	Santa
salute+make+shown) ?	salutation
salute+shown) ?	solution
salvation+aged) ?	salvage
same**+I+are**) ?	similar

sanitary+**eyes**+**di**d) ?	sanitized
sanctuary+**harmony**+**us**+**see**) ?	sanctimoniously
sanctuary+**writ**ten) ?	Sanskrit
Saturns+**day**) ?	Saturday
sat+**hold**) ?	saddle
save+**flavor**) ?	savor
save+i+**are**) ?	savior
save+**your**) ?	savior
say+**age**d) ?	sage
say+**di**d) ?	said
scraped+**jamm**ed+**bal**led ?	scrambled
scar+**stab**) ?	scab
scene+**area**+**be**) ?	scenery
scene+**narr**ow) ?	scenario
scent+**sexual**) ?	sensual
schedule+**the**me) ?	scheme
scour+**sa**ve+**avenge**) ?	scavenge
scrape+**rub**) ?	scrub
scream+**spe**ech) ?	screech
screech+**hawk**) ?	squawk
screech+**talk**) ?	squawk
scribble+**crypti**c) ?	script
scribble+**draw**) ?	scrawl
scribble+**pictures**) ?	scriptures
scribe+**dri**bble) ?	scribbles
scribed+**rolls**) ?	scrolls
sealed+**lips**) ?	silence
seat+**dent**+**make**) ?	sedate
secret+**are**+**be**) ?	secretary
secret+**quest**+**there**+**di**d) ?	sequestered
secure+**of**+**thee**) ?	security
set+**make**) ?	sedate
sedate+**very**) ?	sedentary
see+**all**) ?	saw
see+been) ?	seen
seed+**low**) ?	sow
see+**ess**ence) ?	sense
see+**how**) ?	sow
seek+**cure**) ?	secure
seek+**election**) ?	selection
seek+**got**) ?	sought
seek+**right**) ?	secret
see+**one**) ?	Son
see+**peek**) ?	seek

seeps+**wet**) ?	sweat
see**k**+**quest**) ?	secrets
see+**un**der) ?	Sun
seize+Czar/T**zar**) ?	Caesar
sell+**old**) ?	sold
sense+**nil**) ?	senile
senses+**all**) ?	sensual
sent+**intimate**) ?	sentiment
sent+**utterance**) ?	sentences
sequestered+**rituals**) ?	secrets
sequestered+**writes**) ?	secrets
Serapis+elo**him**) ?	seraphim
serene+**made**) ?	serenade
sere**ne**+**tone**+**in**) ?	serotonin
sere**ne**+**rap**hsody+**is**) ?	Serapis
serpentine+**repetitious**) ?	surreptitious
serpent+**reptiles**+**is**+**sh**own) ?	surreptitious
ser**ve**+**man**) ?	sermon
sew+**low**) ?	sown
sew+**pinch**) ?	cinch
shabby+**odd**+be) ?	shoddy
shade+bel**ow**) ?	shadow
shade+**man**) ?	shaman
shade+**name**) ?	shame
shadow+**rounded**) ?	shrouded
shade+sh**ow**) ?	shadow
shad**y**+**low**+be) ?	shadowy
shake+qu**iver**) ?	shiver
shake+**rift**) ?	shift
shake+**sift**) ?	shift
shaky+fl**abby**) ?	shabby
shall+**care**) ?	share
Shambala+**om**) ?	Shalom
shame+g**ood**) ?	should
shame+**scam** ?	sham
shamesh+**man**) ?	Shaman
Shamash+**one**) ?	sun
sha**ve**+**near**) ?	shear
sheep+**herd**er) ?	shepherd
sheep+pe**ople**) ?	sheeple
shell+**there**) ?	shelter
shell+**wool**) ?	shawl
shelf+h**older**) ?	shoulder
shift+**aft**) ? sh**ove**+**aft**) ?	shaft

shine+**how**) ?	shows
shine+k**now**) ?	show
shine+m**ade**) ?	shade
shine+s**een**) ?	sheen
shoe+gro**ove**) ?	shove
shore+l**ay**) ?	surely
sh**oulder**+c**loud**) ?	shroud
sh**oulder**+**wool**) ?	shawl
shout+**creak**) ?	shriek
sh**ove**+good) ?	should
sh**ove**+**hole**) ?	shovel
sh**ove**+**hoe**) ?	shoe
sh**ove**+**toe**) ?	shoe
sh**ove**+lift) ?	shift
sh**ow**+**all**) ?	shall
sh**ow**+g**ood**) ?	Should could
shot+**sit**) ?	shit
shriek+squ**eal**) ?	shrill
shun+**aimed**) ?	shamed
shut+her) ?	shutters
sickle+**cy**cle+kni**fe**) ?	scythe
si**g**nal+hi**gh**) ?	sigh
sign+**all**) ?	signal
si**milar**+**metric+all**) ?	symmetrical
si**milar**+**name**+in) ?	synonym
si**milar**+**name**) ?	same
si**milar**+t**ool**) ?	symbol
sin+**l**+**stir**/store) ?	sinister
sin+**phallus**) ?	syphilis
sin+**theos**+make) ?	synthetic
sip+g**oop**) ?	soup
sire+**us**) ?	Sirius
sit+**dent**+**very**) ?	sedentary
sit+**led**) ?	settled
sit+you+make+**shown**) ?	situation
skull+a**perture**) ?	sculpture
s**lide**+**bed**) ?	sled
s**lide**+di**ced**) ?	sliced
s**lide**+**hurry**) ?	slurry
s**lip**+**deep**) ?	sleep
s**lop**+**loose**) ?	slue
s**low**+bl**ob**) ?	slob
s**low**+**deep**) ?	sleep
s**lurry**+**juice**) ?	sluice

smack+crash) ?	smash
small+push) ?	smush
small+wack) ?	smack
smash+other) ?	smother
smite+axe ?	smack
smolther+choke) ?	smoke
smoke+foggy) ?	smoggy
smoke+inhale) ?	smell
smoke+melted) ?	smelted
smoke+other) ?	smother
smush+trash) ?	smash
snag+catch) ?	snatch
snake+peek) ?	sneak
snake+seek) ?	sneak
snake+vipers) ?	snipers
snatch+drag) ?	snag
sneak+act) ?	snack
sneers+flicker) ?	snicker
snide+jeers) ?	sneers
snip+clap) ?	snip
snob+bark) ?	snark
snob+hide) ?	snide
snoot+out) ?	snout
snout+breeze) ?	sneeze
snout+got) ?	snot
snout+roar) ?	snore
snot+blow) ?	snow
snub+noble) ?	snob
snub+objective) ?	snob
soaked+boggy)	soggy
soft+cry) ?	sigh
some+body) ?	somebody
songs+calm) ?	psalms
son+hole) ?	soul
soft+smoothing) ?	soothing
solar+celebration) ?	Solabration
Sol+celebrate+shown) ?	Solabration
solemn+attitude) ?	solitude
Sol+star) ?	Solar
Sol+om+on) ?	Solomon
Sol+stop) ?	solstice
sorrow+had) ?	sad
sorry+woe) ?	sorrow
soul+of+man) ?	Solomon

sound+**ringing**) ?	singing
source+see) ?	sorcery
source+seer) ?	sorcerer
sou**th**+**force**) ?	source
South+**turn**) ?	southern
sow+**out**+**the**os/theta)	South
Sow+**un**der) ?	Sun
s**p**ace+**lot**) ?	spot
speak+**reach**) ?	speech
speak+**tell**) ?	spells
s**p**ear+**arrow**) ?	sparrow
s**p**ew+**it**) ?	spit
s**p**ill+**end**) ?	spend
s**p**ill+**g**erm) ?	sperm
s**p**ill+**oil**ed) ?	spoils
s**p**irit+**all**+s**w**ir**ling**) ?	spiraling
s**p**irit+**light**) ?	sprite
s**p**it+**arc**) ?	spark
s**p**it+chew) ?	spew
s**p**it**+to**+in) ?	spittoon
s**p**irit+**kooky**) ?	spooky
s**p**ot+**eye**) ?	spy
s**p**ot+**places**) ?	spaces
s**p**ot+**poof**) ?	spoof
s**p**ray+**ark**) ?	spark
s**p**raying+tw**inkling**) ?	sprinkling
s**p**read+**pain**) ?	sprain
s**p**ring+**air**) **?**	spear
s**p**ring+**flung**) ?	sprung
s**p**ring+**lights**) ?	sprites
s**p**ring+**out**) ?	sprout
s**p**ring+**pain**) ?	sprain
s**p**ring+tw**igs**) ?	sprigs
s**p**rout+**ray**) ?	spray
s**p**ice+fr**eckles**) ?	speckles
s**p**y+**hider**) ?	spider
s**q**ueal+**creak**) ?	squeak
s**q**ueeze+sma**sh**) ?	squish
s**q**uiggle+**worm**) ?	squirm
s**uck**+**in**) ?	sink
s**uck**s+**lips**) ?	sips
s**uck**+**un**der) ?	sunk
s**ub**+**lim**it+**minimal**) ?	subliminal
s**ub**merse+**glued**) ?	subdued

summit+rea**lized**) ?	summarized
summit+re**peat**) ?	Summer
sure+**g**o) ?	surge
surge+**on**) ?	surgeon
survey+**veil**+**acts**) ?	surveillance
Surya+**end**+un**der** ?	surrender
suspicious+in**spect**) ?	suspect
ST) ?	**Stop**
stall+**lion**) ?	stallion
staff+**tilt**) ?	stilt
stand+**up**) ?	stump
stay+**able**) ?	stable
stay+**op**pose) ?	stop
steal+weal**th**) ?	stealth
steep+**t**em**ple**) ?	steeple
stench+d**ank**) ?	stank
stench+**funk**) ?	stunk
step+**air**) ?	stairs
step+**romp**) ?	stomp
stick+**out**) ?	stout
stick+**poke**) ?	stoke
sticks+sn**ake**) ?	stake
stink+**trench**) ?	stench
stole+**cache**) ?	stash
stop+**able**) ?	stable
stop+**age**) ?	stage
stop+**at**) ?	state
stop+d**ance**)	stance
stop+**far**) ?	star
stop+**or**ate) ?	store
stout+pu**dgy**) ?	stodgy
stop+**virility**) ?	sterility
store+be**low**) ?	stow
store+**see**) ?	story
story+**cage**) ?	storage
straight+**roll**) ?	stroll
strain+**anger**) ?	stranger
strain+**juggle**) ?	struggle
strain+**saddle**) ?	straddled
strangling+ch**oke**) ?	stroke
strap+**reign**) ?	strain
streak+**straight**) ?	street
stretch+**pain**) ?	strain
stride+**roll**) ?	stroll

string+dru**mmer**) ?	strummer
string+**hum**) ?	strum
strip+**puppet**) ?	strumpet
strong+**pain**) ?	strain
stroll+aw**ay**) ?	stray
strong+m**angle**) ?	strangle
strong+**theos**) ?	strength
strong+wr**ap**) ?	strap
strum+**ring**) ?	string
strut+g**lide**) ?	stride
strut+r**oll**) ?	stroll
suck+**lip**) ?	sip
sub**ducted+merged**) ?	submerged
suffer+**o**+making) ?	suffocating
Summer+Aryans) ?	Sumerians
Sun+wisdom) ?	Sunwise
super+**pressing**) ?	suppressing
surface+**vi**tal+**live**) ?	survive
sus**pect**+**i**+**see**+of+**us**) ?	suspicious
sus**pence+end**) ?	suspend
suture+eme**rgency**) ?	surgery
s**way**+b**ag**) ?	swag
s**way**+c**urve**) ?	swerve
s**way**+st**agger**) ?	swagger
s**way**+wi**ggle**) ?	swiggle
s**wear**+**word**) ?	sword
s**wine**+han**dle**) ?	swindle
s**wi**nging+w**ay**) ?	sway
s**wing**+wi**pe**) ?	swipe
s**wi**sh+cur**ling**) ?	swirling
s**wi**sh+wi**pe**) ?	swipe
s**word**+pra**yer**) ?	swear
s**worn**+h**ear**) ?	swear
symbol+symbio**tic**) ?	symbolic
syncronistic+**links**) ?	syncs
T) ?	**At, Cross**
ta**boo+ooze**) ?	booze
tacky+char) ?	tar
talk+**each**) ?	teach
talk+**tell**) ?	tale
talk+th**ought**) ?	taught
t**alk+trail**) ?	tell
Tao+all) ?	dual
tear+**able**) ?	terrible

taste+**ess**ence) ?	test
teet+n**ip**) ?	Tip tit
tell+a+**vision**) ?	television
tell+**scope**) ?	telescope
ten**t**+**pole**) ?	temple
terror+**able**) ?	terrible
test+ate) ?	taste
they+**ev**ils) ?	thieves
they+**leave**) ?	thief
theos+**ought**) ?	thought
theta+**ought**) ?	thought
they+lift/left) ?	theft
Thors+**day**) ?	Thursday
Thor+**under**) ?	thunder
thought+**link**) ?	think
thought+**tinker**) ?	thinker
through+**live**) ?	thrive
thump+d**ud**) ?	thud
till+s**oil**) ?	toil
tinge+tick**le**) ?	tingle
to+**gather**) ? **two**+**gather**) ?	together
to+hole) ?	tool
tonal+h**oots**) ?	toots
tool+s**oil**) ?	toil
to+**tal**ly) ?	total
tot+j**oy**) ?	toy
tot+wad**dler**) ?	toddler
trade+**ash**) ?	trash
trade+**sure**) ?	treasure
tra**gic**+d**rama**) ?	trauma
tramp+**ash**) ?	trash
trance+**quell**) ?	tranquil
transfer+in**scriptions**) ?	transcriptions
transfer+**jet**+story) ?	trajectory
transfer+**port**) ?	transport
trans**port**+**holes**) ?	portals
travel+**up**) ?	trump
treasure+**eat**) ?	treat
trick+sn**ap**) ?	trap
trip+**eat**) ?	treat
true+**sure**) ?	treasure
true+stop) ?	trust
true+**thought**) ?	truth
True+**us**+at) ?	trust

truth+sayer) ?	soothsayer
Try+fail) ?	trivail
try+umph) ?	triumph
tuff+c**urd**) **?**	turd
turmoil+you+relent) ?	turbulent
tw**isted+light**) ?	twilight
twice+**st**op) ?	twist
twice+w**ink+**able) ?	twinkle
twist+c**urling**) ?	twirling
twist+s**eeking**) ?	tweaking
twist+sw**irl) ?**	twirl
twist+wh**irling**) ?	twirling
U) ?	**Up or Under**
umbra+**el**evated+**A**bove) ?	umbrella
under+taker) ?	undertaker
unique+**one**) ?	union
uni**q**ue+**verse**) ?	Universe
unite+**are+i+am**) ?	Unitarian
unit+tie) ?	unity
uni**ty+verse**) ?	universes
univer**s**e+**all**) ?	universal
universal+city) ?	university
U+no)+down) ?	under
not+**c**ultured+**truth**) ?	uncouth
up+common+make) ?	accommodate
up+ease) ?	appease
up+heal) ?	appeal
up+**sce**ne+**b**end) ?	ascend
up+**spire**+make+**shown**) ?	aspiration
V) ?down, woman~ voman	**Victor, Down, woman~voman**
vacant+sees) ?	vacancies
vacate+**shown**) ?	vacations
val**i**ant+**true**) ?	value
value+able) ?	valuable
vege**t**able+ag**rarian**) ?	vegetarian
ver**b+boas**t) ?	verbose
ver**ily+true**) ?	virtue
vib**e+rate**) ?	vibrate
vib**r**ate+**act**) ?	vibrant
vib**ra**tion+c**h**ant) ?	vibrant
victor+s**tory**) ?	victory
vic**t**ory+**tim**id) ?	victim
vile+m**an**) ?	villain
vile+st**age**) ?	village

vine+**age**) ?	vintage
violet+lance) ?	violence
virtue+**us**) ?	virtuous
vis**u**al+**ares**) ?	Wizard wizards visars advisars
vital+**littles**) ?	vittles
vital+**mini**mums) ?	vitamins
vocal+**you**+dictio**nary**) ?	vocabulary
voice+**call**+i+**is**) ?	vocalizes
volume+**lump**+you+**is**) ?	voluptuous
vow+**ele**vate) ?	vowels
W) ? double V	**Wonder Question, Wise, Wit**
wade+**low**) ?	wallow
war+inform) ?	warn
woe+sorry) ?	worry
wave+wind) ?	wand
wear+torn)**?**	worn
we+eat) ?	wheat
well+come) ?	welcome
wet+seeps) ?	weeps
wet+there) ?	weather
whores+moan) ?	hormonal
what+end) ?	when
What+there) ?	where
What+human) ?	whom
What+choose) ? change chi	which
What+I) ? of ides of devide into sides	whY a Y is two choices
wheel+curling) ?	whirling
whip+curling) ?	whirling
whizards at+seek) ask)	when, where, which, who, why
whirl+old) ?	world
wholly+sum) ?	wholesome
why+at) ?	what
why+eyes) ?	whise
why+mine+wing) ?	whining
wide+to+hold) ?	width
wild+repeat+essence) ?	wilderness
wild+seeds) ? wee+woods) ?	weeds
wince+blink) ?	wink
wind+norm) ?	warm
wind+turn) ?	winter
wise+ares)?	wizard
wise+dome) ?	wisdom
wide+size)	wise
wise+word) ?	whisord

wise+orate+did) ?	word
wise+wh**ords**)	whizard
wish+ve**sper**) ?	whisper
wit+**change**) ?	wish
wit+**change**+**craft**) ?	witchcraft
wit+**there**) ? **when**+**there**) ?	whether
wild+**seeds**) ? wild+**reeds**) ?	weeds
will+g**ood**) ?	would
woe+s**orry**) ?	worry
womb+**man**) ?	woman
wonder+**either**) ?	whether
wonder+**end**) ?	when
wonder+**here**) ?	where
working+**out**side) ?	workout
worm+squi**ggle**) ?	wiggle
worn+t**eary**) ?	weary
woven+**weeds**) **?** **woven**+**reeds**) **?**	weaved
w**rap**+cap**ture**) ?	rapture
w**rith**+do**ing**) ?	writing
w**rith**+drum) ?	rhythm
w**rith**ing+in) ?	rhythm
X) ?	**Intersection**
x+**at**+real**ly**) ?	Exactly, Actually, Factually
X+mas ?	Christ/Chi/Change Mass
Y) ? end of the word Y is choice	**Yes. Why**
yum+**eat**) ? me+**eat**) ?	meat
ye+is) ?	yes
yes+**point**/**pole**] ?	yep
Z) ?	**The end**
Zen+i+**theta** ?	zenith
Zomb+**be**) ?	**Z**ombie
zoo+**ark**) ?	zodiac

Index

155

More Books of K. Sabota
Natures Calendar-Clock: The Divine Design of Time
& Companion Cards: Natures Calendar Cards
The Hidden Sword: A Puzzle Poem Myst Story
Langmythics: Language Mystery Theos
Mathmatics. & Companion Book to
The Hidden Power of Letters A to Z Card Game.
Available on Amazon, ebay or NaturesCalendar.org
Youtube Channel NaturesCalendar